Pit Sense versus the State

A history of militant miners in the Doncaster area

David John Douglass

Pit Sense versus the State
A history of militant miners in the Doncaster area
David John Douglass

Phoenix Press
PO Box 824
London
N1 9DL

0 948984 26 0

Typeset by San Fairy Ann
Printed and bound by BPCC Wheatons

Contents

Dedication

This book is dedicated:-

to the late Brian Croutcher, comrade and fellow Hatfield miner and tireless picket in the 84/85 strike,

to Jack (Geordie) Main, of the pickets' kitchen and welfare team,

to George (Bant) Hardy, Geordie born picket veteran of 21, 26, the 30s, 69, 72, 74, and 84/85,

to the young Donny pitlads who took the tiger by the tail.

Prologue

Since the first decade of its inception the Doncaster coalfield has been at the heart of inspired militant action. It has been quite consistently so, from the the times of the first pits being sunk, and their subsequent staffing with emigrant miners from the older established coalfields, markedly those of Northumberland, Durham and Scotland. Many a blacklisted collier made his way south to find a new pit, where managers starved of manpower turned a blind eye to the 'red ragging' reputation and staffed their pits with itinerant militant miners. In the turbulent days of the general strike the Doncaster miners blazed a trail subsequently followed quite literally by their sons and grandsons.

Many readers will notice disturbing parallels with that more recent event — the miners' strike of 1984 to 1985. These parallels are not coincidental. In the 1920s and again in the 1970s and 1980s the coal mines were the chief battleground of the class war. Then as now the leaders of the miners were tough and determined. They had to be for the mine owners were equally tough. It is almost uncanny to discover that many of the incidents of 1926 were repeated, often at the very same locations in the 1980s. (1) It might be added that in the case of at least one aud Geordie lad it was carried out by the same bloke! (see the dedication).

By 1926 the Doncaster coalfield was home to 30,000 miners and their families, but we were far more numerous overall. In May 1926 one million miners struck to resist the imposition of a wage cut and an increase in hours. Blacklegging in Doncaster was extremely rare in 1926, it was little more than 1% by the last week of the 84/85 strike. . . .the strongest coalfield in Britain. In 26 10,000 non-miners struck work in sympathy, many without being 'called out' by the TUC.

All means of transport in and around Doncaster are entirely suspended. There is not a single train or bus of any description running. (2)

To the state, the 26 general strike was the harbinger of a workers' revolution, this was everything contrary to bourgeois political theory and constitution. Here the workers, not in a political party, but in trade union organisations, were challenging the government and the law makers. The TUC leaders liked it no more than the government and had no intention of forming any potential revolutionary government. The police were beginning to get their head, the number of arrests was starting to increase, anti-police sentiment among the pickets began to increase. The police were adopting the attitude that any picket holding his hand up to indicate that a lorry should should stop was illegal. . . .*two Edlington miners were convicted for 'restricting traffic' when they spoke to the driver of a brewer's lorry in the street.* (3)

The conflict again posed itself in 84. *The strike organisation was beginning to face a crucial question over the conduct of the dispute. In essence this was, should rigid picketing be mounted or should union members merely abstain from work.* Much of this was to focus on the government's strike breaking efforts . . . .*as they substituted massive road transport to counter the crippling effects of the virtual shutdown of the railways.* (4)

The response of the miners was to deploy surveillance and interception squads to cover the area's main roads, this in turn led to the deployment of mass pickets and *inevitably led to serious disturbances and violent clashes with the police.*

The worst incident took place at Hatfield on May 12th. A thousand men, mostly miners, had blocked the road with the aid of a large tree trunk. At one point vehicles stretched for several hundred yards along the highway. A newspaper van had been overturned and set on fire. . . .When a large contingent of police, some on horseback, arrived, they were met by a hail of stones and other missiles. The police replied with a baton charge and hand to hand fighting ensued. . . .more than seventy arrests were made.

Another major incident had occurred earlier the same day at Edenthorpe on Thorne Road. A crowd of three hundred pickets had assembled near a junction and were attempting to stop all traffic. A lorry driver had been hauled from his cab and roughed up. A detachment of police arrived on the scene and broke up the picket. Some resistance was made and about twelve pickets were arrested.

We are told that the chairman of the Stainforth strike committee received an additional £20 fine. . . .*because he was identified as a ringleader of the Hatfield fracas.*

6

The Doncaster pickets in 26 appear to have had a great deal of autonomous direction, as they were to assume in later years. The strength of their challenge continued, whilst that of others softened. . . .*outside Doncaster. . . .miners and others stopped blocking traffic by mass pickets. . . .but being without a controlling force to direct their attacks and to withdraw at the right moment, came into unequal conflict with the police and suffered heavily.* (5)

The authorities in their mortal fear of the communist insurgents sought out local leaders, particularly those on the left. A Mr Squeers, the local organiser for ASLEF, was such a man. A member of the local Communist Party he was arrested and charged under section 34 of the Emergency Regulation *inciting people to do an act calculated to impede traffic.* He had addressed a mass meeting in Stainforth and urged everyone to stop all scab vehicles (except those carrying bread or milk). Showing the ongoing political bias of the British courts he was fined £50 and received a three month prison sentence. (6)

Hatfield was clearly a hot bed of sedition and in the round up of political activists a Hatfield collier was charged with the serious offence of 'an act likely to cause disaffection among the police force'. This had happened when three cops had arrived at his home in connection with the rioting at Hatfield Colliery. *You are only human, the same as myself. We are the same flesh and blood. Why don't you join us and rule yourselves? The world was given to the people, not to a select few. I want to see you come with us, we can rule without a king. I have lived under two republics and shall live under one in this country yet, and may God speed the day when we live under labour rule and the workers who are the producers govern the country.*
(Mr Purvis, Hatfield communist miner).

What effect such a subversive and poetic invitation had on PC Joe Soap we don't know, but the senior officer recognised this sort of stuff and decided to suppress all such revolutionary ideas and movements. Disaffection within the police force (and the armed forces) was a real fear for the state and they wished to come down hard against it. The senior magistrate, a Hatfield magistrate, classed Purvis as clearly a dangerous individual with 'extreme opinions'. He was jailed for three months hard labour and fined £100, both the maximum penalties the law would allow. (7)

Walentowicz tells us there seems to have been a deliberate campaign in Doncaster to apprehend and punish those thought to hold 'extreme' political opinions, or those thought 'responsible' for the disturbances. (8)

The spirit of Doncaster resistance does not seem to have been easily extinguished. An Oxford undergraduate, who had come north to Hull to do his patriotic duty scabbing on the docks in Hull, was attacked by stone throwing Doncaster pickets as well as facing attempts to puncture his tyres. Police were attacked at Edlington and a lorry driver at Hatfield. A miner was convicted of an assault on a porter at Arksey station who had refused to join the strike. The court was interested to know 'if he was a communist'. (9)

Throughout the Second World War labour was supposedly solidly behind the patriotic war effort, strikes weren't supposed to happen, they were tantamount to treason and subject to severe legal penalty. Not only this but, following the invasion of the USSR by the Nazis the Communist Party and all of its working class activists and labour lieutenants became wedded to the war effort. Strikes were 'counter revolutionary'. Notwithstanding this solid front of anti-strike propaganda, and despite genuine anti-fascist sentiment among the working class and the miners in particular, the workers refused to give up the struggle for their own cause at home.

YEAR	Total no. of disputes	No. in coal	% in coal
1939	940	404	43.0%
1940	922	38	41.3%
1941	1,25	1470	37.6%
1942	1,303	526	40.4%
1943	1,795	843	47.2%
1944	2,194	1,253	57.1%
1945	2,293	1,306	56.9%
1946	2,205	1,329	60.3%

In the Yorkshire coalfield, and Doncaster within the South Yorkshire area, strikes were endemic. At Hatfield the pit struck, for example, when a female clerk was discovered carrying a box of soap over to the management offices. The miners had been severely cut back on provision of soap, something which was, of course, a vital necessity. Management were creaming the rations off for themselves, the result was a determined wildcat.

Letter from Robert Clive, Secretary, South Yorkshire Coalowners' Association, to Major Lloyd George, Minister of Fuel and Power, 18th June 1942.

I am requested by the South Yorkshire Coalowners' Association to draw your attention to the large number of sporadic strikes which have occurred at several collieries in the district since about the 19th May and which are still taking place.

25 South Yorkshire collieries have been affected and the loss of output has been considerable.

These strikes mainly originate by the boys refusing to work without having made any previous complaint either through their union or direct to management.

In a few cases sabotage of haulage machinery has been reported and every effort has been made to trace the offenders, without success.

The strikers are not supported by the union and the union officials both locally and from the head office of the YMWA have taken energetic steps to keep the pits at work, but with only a limited amount of success and strikes continue to occur. Two large collieries are reported on strike today.

I am desired to ask if the ministry will consider the desirability of taking any action within their power which will effectively curtail these unofficial strikes and consequent loss of production.

The end of the war ushered in great expectations among the people, having disposed of one set of despots there was a ground swell of feeling that despots at home should also go by the same means. It was against this climate that a Labour government, with the most radical progamme in its history, was elected by a landslide vote. Churchill, a man the people were said to have idealised, not only didn't form a government, he lost his own seat as an MP. The Labour government set about the first portion of its plan to take big business into 'common ownership'. One of the chief targets was the mines.

'The Mines for the Miners' had been a slogan of the miners for nearly half a century, the philosophy that the miners should take control of the pits and run them for the benefit of the community had been a watch-word of the miners in the 1830s and right through their fiery involvment with the Chartist movement in the decades that followed. Later there had been primitive attempts at mining workers' co-operatives with the union buying and operating at least one Durham mine. As it turned out this Labour nationalisation was not like any of them. The same 'gaffers' remained, the commercial strategy of the industry was to subsidise private industry, not undermine it. However, nationalisation brought great strides forward in safety, welfare and training. It also enmeshed the NUM in a paternalist swamp of joint arbitration boards, conciliation and consultation bodies and an ideology that linked the union cheek by jowl to 'the industry', the pits were 'ours', managed by the NCB in co-operation with the NUM. The early years through the 50s ensured that at national level at least we scarce had a separate identity. We could do nothing that would damage the industry or its image, we dared not push in our own cause for fear of damaging the tender fledgling. (10)

The suffocating bureaucratic 'Labour shit doesn't stink' philosophy of the offical NUM leadership had hogtied the union since the late 50s in such a fatalistic grip that many in the industry thought if we weren't already dead we were sort of undead. The industry was washed out, doomed, the skills of the miners long since redundant, many parts of Britain thought of coal mines purely a a thing of the 20s and 30s and had no idea as to the still vast extent of the industry, despite the monumental devastation at the hands of 'labour man' Lord Robens. We were feeling the white hot heat of the modern technology Wilson had told us about, and suddenly the accepted labour of the miner in the thin seams of the north and west became a crusade to 'bring the poor miners laying in cramped spaces back into the fresh air'. The cramped spaces in which we had worked collectively for two centuries and more were none the less cramped for the passage of time, but were made all the more unacceptable by the knowledge that among British low paid workers, we were among the very lowest. The forgotten industry. 'Are there still coal mines up north?' a railway porter asked incredulously as we massed for the grand demonstration in London in 67. We had been pushed so far even the leadership in its most rightwing mode since the end of the 19th century had felt the whip of indifference. Sir Sidney Ford, the union's President, had urged the government 'to think again' whilst Mr Paynter, the union's Secretary, apologised for having to oppose the government's fuel policy but 'felt compelled'. The Labour government's fascination with nuclear energy was such that it fell over itself in a mad rush to close the mines 'on behalf of the poor miners' and install nuclear power stations, (presumably for the benefit of the poor uranium miners) to supply a 'cheap fuel' economy. At the same time the first of the fuel privatisations had begun (in 67) with North Sea gas going at once into the hands of the speculative and thoroughly individualistic private companies. Paynter complained 'We accept concentration of the industry ("concentration" was later replaced by "rationalisation") but the rundown is taking the industry to the very point of disintegration'. In an even more cringing tract he urged that 'It is just not possible for any government to deal with the human problems in such a short space of time.' The pit closure programme should be slowed down!

Amazing that we only discovered the closure of uneconomic pits was a Tory dogma, whilst in actual fact at the mass rally at the Central Hall, Westminster, a radical thought had been projected. The Morning Star of 7th November 67 reported 'Even uneconomic pits should be kept open in order to retain a reservoir of labour for new industries which might be brought in.'

The Labour establishment thought coal mines and socialism red in tooth an anachronism and because the coal industry itself was an anachronism fighting for its very survival any talk of wage rises was treachery. Any talk of shortening hours was stabbing 'the industry' in the back at a time when it needed all the co-operation it could get from the miners, ie continued poverty wages and hours still the legacy of the 26 defeat, at least as far as surfacemen were concerned.

Other voices thought differently, a new breed of young miner was emerging, very much in step with his rock and revolution generation despite the isolation of the pit villages and the predominance of traditional cloth capped culture. The unofficial movement which began to emerge from a hundred strands around the country wasn't a unified voice at first and ran from wage militancy on one hand to revolutionary miners' factions in Doncaster on the other. The irons were already in the fire as Cadeby launched its dramatically important strike in September 69 over 'market men's' wage rates. This was not simply a dispute over the establishment of a fall back rate for surplus face men, but the very corner of job control and union manning. When the Board dug their toes in, the flying pickets spread their wings, Goldthorpe being the

11

first of the Doncaster collieries out in solidarity. A mass picket and lobby streamed from the collieries to Manvers, South Yorkshire's Area HQ. Cortonwood, Manvers, Kilnhurt, Barnburgh, Maltby, Wath and Goldthorpe were all out with Cadeby, and the Doncaster branches waited in the wings, in the traditional tactic of stopping your own area first before moving off to picket out others. The dispute was met with widespread success, and whet the appetite of Yorkshire miners for the forthcoming struggles.

Following the unoffical lobby and rally in London, called by Derbyshire, the immediate focus of action became the question of surfacemens' hours, an extended day which we had carried since the defeat in 26 and which meant in effect that surface workers were paid only for 8 hours' work, whilst their 'snap' break of half an hour was unpaid. A reduction of hours was the unifying demand as South Wales, Yorkshire, Scotland and Derbyshire stopped work in the first co-ordinated but quite unofficial national action since the 26 strike itself. As pickets spread throughout the country Durham pits resisted dire warnings of disciplinary action from the Red Hills offices and struck, as did the Lancashire collieries when the Yorkshire pickets arrived. In shades of things to come, the Nottingham coalfield seen vigilante groups of women riding 'shotgun' on their husbands to ensure they went to work. Quite a few of the hardy Doncaster pickets felt a rap round the lug with a frying pan as they tried to encourage the Nottingham men to cease work. But the strike took all before it, with many Nottingham collieries stopping as firmly as Yorkshire. Meantime the more constitutional of the Doncaster miners were in London to lobby that the NEC make the strike official. Angry rank and file miners ensured that NEC members had to press their way through to their meeting. More than a few were already beginning to feel the wind of change. The unofficial action didn't succeed at first push, but the wage demand was met in full, something which had never happened before. Three years later the impact of that victory fully registered upon the bulk of the rank and file, the miners still had power, and if we still had bargaining clout, why were we bottom of the wages league?

The strike of 69 was first blood for a new generation of miners, in excess of 40% of Britain's pits were at a standstill. Coal merchants had never held stock, had never believed stocks would dry up, the impact was immediate as neither gas works nor power stations had built up any reserve supply. By October the 21st the strike was still solid in Yorkshire with above 70,000 men on strike, but the day after, by 14 votes to 5, the NEC recommended acceptance of the wages offer and an end to the negotiations. This prompted pits in South Wales to return and the Lancashire pits to go back also. When the recommendation was put in Yorkshire it was rejected by 80 votes to 8 and a resolution to carry forward the strike was passed. Yorkshire was then joined by the Kent men and some of the Lancashire pits were picketed back out. Meantime the number of pits stood in Scotland reached 14 with 4 more coming out after the NEC recommendation than had previously been involved in the action. 2 more came out in Derbyshire leaving only 2 working in the whole of that county.

The strike failed initially at least to wring concessions on payment for surfacemens' 'snap' or reduce their hours instead; but the action, loosely co-ordinated by a mostly unoffical leadership of militants and revolutionaries, mainly the former, set the stage for the minority view that 'action pays dividends' to become the majority and surging view, enough to carry forward the later strikes which rattled a government. More still, the more constitutional tacticians defeated the right wing and severely dinted the bureacracy with changes in the strike rule from a two thirds majority to one of 55%. Certainly later strikes could not have been carried out (officially) without these important victories.

Notes

1 The General Strike in Doncaster, May 1926. PJ Walentowicz
2 TUC General Council Intelligence Report, 11th May 1926. W Paling
3 Walentowicz, op cit p11
4 op cit p11
5 A Workers' history of the Great Strike. RW Postgate, E Wilkinson, MF and PJF Horrabin, p44
6 Walentowicz, op cit p13
7 Doncaster Gazette, May 21st 1926
8 Walentowicz, op cit p14
9 ibid
10 Of course this paternalism worked both ways, coal industry management were frequently bred and born from the pit communities, some had started on the face, others had families still at the pick point. It left a paternalist tradition which drove MacGregor wild when he arrived to

do the pits and their unions down. 'Joint consultation' was not a feature of his vocabulary, he hated 'soft' management quite as much as strong unions, his was the industrial relations of Pol Pot.

14

The Doncaster Pickets

Years of picketing experience and custom had taught Yorkshire miners that the following process would be followed when asking for support. If a face ragged up, you generally waited until all the other shifts on that face ragged up before the pit was laid idle. The pit would itself be on strike for a fortnight or so before picketing out other pits in your panel area. Your own panel would stand entirely before going into other panel areas, and finally your own county would be stood before you went over county borders.

When the strike started we were by no means 100% certain that York-shire would stand without encouragement from pickets. There had been rebellious rumblings from the north of the county and the York-shire pits bordering Notts and Derbyshire. True to tradition we resolved to concentrate on weak spots in our own county before going over into Notts or elsewhere.

Thus it was that on the morning of March 12th pickets were massed in Welfare centres all over Doncaster, itching to get into action and waiting for the order from Brodsworth to 'go'.

There had never been a question as to whether pickets would be deployed, only when. The perspective of the strike centres was to consolidate Yorkshire, give Notts the chance to bring itself out, but if they didn't respond to be ready to go over and picket them out, or else assist the Notts pickets where they needed help.

A hoary myth has been built up, in the first place by the so called Socialist Workers' Party (SWP) and then repeated unquestioningly by others of the same ilk, that the 'leadership' ie everybody bar them, had no intention of picketing, that without the 'rank and file' intervention and/or the SWP initiative the first pickets would never have been dispatched at all and that the credit for the 'kick start' to the strike was theirs. It is simply not true; the plan was as stated, the strike HQ entry for the first day reads:

All pits stood in Doncaster. Picketing of own collieries. Hatfield picketing Thorne, COSA picketing Coal House and St. Georges.

However, Armthorpe, ever the restless warrior, could not contain its wish to get up and at 'em, and immediately had swept into Nottinghamshire quite as a spontaneous action. They picketed the days and afters shifts and reported 40% of the Harworth men had turned back or joined the line.

In the meantime Doncaster had sent out for pickets for the Doncaster Mines Rescue Station, which it seems everyone had overlooked and nobody had been covering. Hatfield's pickets were at once dispatched. This in turn led to an argument which was to develop as the strike went on. The rescue men insisted that they had been given permission to work by Ken Holmer (Area Financial Secretary) but this hadn't been passed on to the Barnsley co-ordinating centre. With great reluctance we withdrew the pickets.

Elsewhere, Armthorpe pickets had rolled up to Hatfield, Edlington and one or two other welfares and built up their unofficial forces for a mass picket of Harworth that evening.

Harworth for its part was having an emergency meeting that day to vote on whether they should work or not. Brian Connolly had been hurriedly invited to speak at the branch in the hope of swinging support. However, the invitation sent by the Harworth militants wasn't received until 9am. At 10am Harworth voted to work.

As soon as news of this spread, branches and pickets started to lobby for permission to dispatch their pickets to Harworth. The Doncaster HQ passed on the mood to Holmer who in turn promised an emergency EC meeting on the situation.

As soon as it was convened, the meeting discussed the current situation, and after a brief debate the common consensus was that Yorkshire as a whole now swing into action and deploy pickets to every Nottinghamshire pit.

Below decks in the old EC room, the picket maps and targets of ten

16

years earlier were being dug out; extra phones were being installed; incident books drawn up; phone message records, and the whole paraphenalia of a war room was being constructed. Rotas, volunteers, advice and co-ordination, speaker lists, sympathetic trade unions, likely conflict areas, a general hubbub rose to a din with the dense smoke which quickly filled the room. People flying in and out, armfuls of literature, orders, plans.

Our intelligence was not what it should have been. For targets we dug out old colliery year books and ordnance survey maps. With this information we sought targets, it was not always effective, though it was sometimes amusing.

As the co-ordinators ran to their cars or shouted instructions down telephones (a thing we were to avoid later) Doncaster was already targeting its first Nottinghamshire objective.

Carcroft/Winders/Highgate	Bestwood
Armthorpe	Bevercotes/Harworth
Askern	Bilsthorpe
Goldthorpe	Blidworth
Rossington	Calverton
Hickleton	Clipstone
Brodsworth	Cotgrave/Linby
Frickley	Gedling/Hucknall
Edlington	Newstead
Hatfield	Ollerton
Bentley	Rufford

Soon the responses from the colliery strike centres started to be relayed back, Hatfield would take every available picket tonight and stop through to picket the day shift as well.

Askern pickets gone on three shift cycle to Bilsthorpe.

Then the first of the year book disasters. Bestwood had been closed, but not by the Highgate pickets. It was already shut before they got there and they had moved on to Hucknell.

Armthorpe concentrating all pickets on Bevercotes leaving a token force at Harworth.

17

Edlington phoned in, requested assistance at Newstead, as did High-gate who had encountered bus loads of police at Hucknell.

By 10.10 pm the first successes were being phoned in.

Goldthorpe had stopped the Blidworth night shift and had been redeployed to Newstead and Hucknell to assist our branches requesting help.

Hickleton, 3/4 of Clipstone night shift returned home.

Hatfield, police were drawn from Ollerton to some big push they were making at Thornby (a South Yorkshire target), subsequently Ollerton night shift completely stopped. Departing police had warned, 'We'll be back you lot when we've sorted these out.' Request back up.

Edlington report Newstead night shift turned back, but there were expressions that they will return with the day shift and storm the lines. Request assistance.

To the picket planners there were just never enough pins in the board to meet every request for assistance. It was a juggling act, draw some off here, cut down there, hold off that shift and double up on another.

Hatfield, regardless of the police threat 'to be back', kept its 200 pickets in the field overnight in readiness for the next morning. Meanwhile Armthorpe, Hatfield's closest ally, dispatched all its pickets at midnight to Ollerton to back up the Hatfield men.

By 20 minutes to 1 on Tuesday the second day of action, Doncaster had already started to weedle in other area's pickets to back up its own operations. Silverwood and Cadeby pickets had been asked for and obliged with pickets to back Hickie up at Clipstone.

Brodsworth deployed to back up Armthorpe and Hatfield who report an expected 1,500 men turning up at Ollerton. Brodsworth complain that branch finances are now gone and urgent money is needed to keep pickets going.

In fact this was the message that started to come through as the reality of the situation and the logistics of organisation took the place of the initial enthusiasm.

It should be noted that throughout the first days of the operation in Notts little or no violence was experienced. Pickets confronted fellow miners in much the way they had done for a century or so. Successes were frequent. Like the message received from Hickleton at 2.25 am Tuesday 13th March 'All North Notts pits down, very little police action or interference. Token pickets left on gates.' As the morning went on and the pickets moved from pit to pit the pattern was similar. Most Notts men didn't want to strike particularly, but they didn't want to force the issue and would return home whenever a picket was mounted. It wasn't in fact until someone decided they shall go to work that the bitter chalice was forced to their lips, together with much back-slapping from the establishment and choruses of well dones from the Tory party.

Ollerton

Throughout the morning the police started to build up, and as such all and every spare picket was deployed to back up the lads already down there. Hickleton was sent to join Hatfield, Armthorpe and Brodsworth. Jimmy Miller (Armthorpe Secretary) phoned in to report a mobile police HQ being drafted into Ollerton village, and monitoring of vehicles and picket movements on the motorway.

Successes still carry on coming in:-
Bilsthorpe, night shift out
Frickley report Hucknall out
Goldthorpe report Blidsworth stood
Edlington report Newstead stood
8.25 am Tuesday, Ollerton stood, the whole day shift turned back.

About the same time small numbers of casual arrests are reported and the mechanisms of bail, representation, transport home, information to relatives begin to clank rather than 'swing' into place. By a few days more it would become a highly polished operation.

3.30 pm Calverton men picket their own pit with assistance from our men, all banksmen gone home except one, same with the winders, 50% of the colliery out under their own steam.
9.25 pm Armthorpe/Hatfield report 500 pickets at Ollerton pit gates, all shifts picketed out.

Bentley reports bus driver taking their pickets into action arrested and ignition keys confiscated.

Welsh pickets in action at Moor Green.

By 10.50 pm arrests of leading Hatfield and Armthorpe militants had started at Ollerton, police fail to shift the line.

While the branch voted 20 to 1 to work, 1,000 Doncaster pickets on the gate voted that they would not. Police road blocks being set up to prevent reinforcements for the day shift picket.

The relationship of direction between Barnsley and its banks of telephones and faithful EC members trying to link objectives and the local panel strike HQs around the clock, was to say the least uncertain at this time. The bold objectives were common to both, the finer details, the plugging the gaps, the cries for help, went to Barnsley. The Doncaster panel directors of operations had not yet seized the initiative and as such many demands and requests were passed on to 'Arthur's Castle' for an uncertain future. The question of finance, money to fund operations, loomed large at this time. Barnsley officials still by and large held the purse strings and the purse determined the extent of the plan local or otherwise. In this first week the bulk of the picketing was done for nowt, nowt at least so far as the union was concerned. The pickets themselves funded many of the operations, then came the branch funds. As these expired the question of central funding loomed. How much, to whom and for what? Who would then judge what was to be done and what was to be paid for? As yet these questions did not occupy the bitter stage they were later to hold. The strike was new, the enthusiasm was abounding, the pickets were, as in 74 and 72, rolling all before them.

We were an army of the strike, the pickets and their local HQs. We little contemplated the other aspects of the strike at this time and so it was that wild imaginative initiatives welled up, and were enthusiastically passed on to Barnsley, a source which we knew and understood in ordinary branch activity, but did not know the mechanisms of now. Neither did they. We were no well oiled insurrectionary body sweeping into rebellion. We were a trade union, set in our ways, proud of our past cause, retracing steps we knew, with little thought that the ground had changed and no new structures to tackle it set down. That we have a bureaucracy is as obvious as saying that we are still a trade union. But faults and obstructions that there were, that leadership and structure held true for 12 months intact and in fact changed its character and did gently roll over and allow itself if not to change, never to give in, or confront the bulk of the pickets on the streets. Few union structures in Britain, if any, would have done as much. The miners' union went into action warts and contradictions and all, and held tight to each other despite sometimes furious battles later for direction and control of policy, plans, money and public image. We never split. The people who subsequently scabbed left us from the word go, they never split the union; they actually in all things except name were never really part of it, since the 1940s fusion with Spencer. The evidence had been there for decades.

The imagination of the Brodsworth strike centre was streets in advance in terms of strategy than all other centres. By the third day of the strike it was recommending dynamic policies to overcome the only half formed policies of obstruction being operated by the police. Thus it was that Doncaster sent an urgent request that the rail unions be involved in helping us fill empty freight trains and ship our pickets in by rail to avoid the roads. Either official or otherwise, we would pour out from the freight cars and avoid the blocks. It was preposterous, practical and was an idea of the mettle of the pickets themselves. Nowt more was ever heard of it. As the balance of direction swung later to the panel centres such ideas were acted on directly, although that particular one was pegged.

To be set at the head of the greatest, most dynamic miners in Britain and charged with directing picketing, is in the first flush of position a terrifically ego-boosting situation; it doesn't last. In the coming weeks I was to learn not to sleep, and to realise that lying down on a bed and thinking for three hours wasn't sleep anyway. The brain ran on, the brain set the ears at red alert and listened to any clue of inspiration, the idea that a great plan, a big plan, an imaginative plan, was required on each day; the pride that an operation had got the drop on the police attempts to foil it; the reports coming in of pits 100% stood through solidarity action had to be contrasted to the defeats. In the first weeks I was awarded The Order of the Prick, because of the laying low of collieries which had ceased production and closed years before the strike: 'The good news or the bad news?'
They had phoned through around 10.30 pm.
'Gis the good stuff first,' we replied.
'The pit is 100% closed and the pickets are all in operation, police are confused but non violent.'

21

'Good lads, good lads, what is the bad news?'

'Bad news is it closed some years ago!'

Gulp, and passing of buck, explanations about year books, fighting where we stand, etc. etc., then

'OK, pass onto the nearest pit.'

'Knackers, we've got the fire going, a little tent set up, local people are giving us mugs of tea, the police have camped out in transits all round, they think we know something nobody else does, and we figure while they are with us, they aren't with anybody else, so good night, we'll try again tomorrow Pillocks!'

The second reason was for the direction of men to the wharf to stop the cargo being unloaded. Again the response was 100% success. All loading stopped, cranes threatened with occupation, lorry drivers dumb struck and compliant, total blacking of the cargo by dockers, which turned out to be a kind of brownie black rice and not a kind of brownie black anthracite as reported.

Following the huge and vicious battles with some of the area officials and having been very strongly disciplined for detailed instructions as to how to picket in given situations, a Frickley presentation of a badge saying 'Nobody does it better.' In contrast again, the most agonising was the sending of men to objectives which you yourself would not be at, every report of police attack, every arrest, every case in hospital stung right through to the soul, and guilt, coupled with the contradiction that this was the position I had been given to hold, made for uneasy nights. Someone had to direct the troops, but the rejoinder when anything went wrong or the police prejudged us 'it's alright for you you bastard' stung the heart, along with the immediate recollection of images of officers behind the lines and the troops fighting it out at the front. It was to follow that every time I went 'to the front' and tried to take command from the head of the column, the police closed in within minutes and lifted me. To direct operations in the field from the rear of the operation was worse than doing it from an office, 'why dint yee get stuck in instead of skulking back here wanking it off?'

In this vein the operation at Silverhill cut most of all. It had been drawn up to avoid the police road blocks, to use the benefit of complete surprise and most of all to be successful. As it turned out, either by coincidence, or else by a leak, mounted police were waiting in the fields as the lads set off across open ground. Despite repeated charges the lads kept on coming and got to the pit very much the worse for batterings. Two of these lads came to the strike HQ fuming with anger and accusation. One poor bloke, his head gashed right down the middle, hard caked blood down his forehead, asked which 'stupid bastard had set that up today?' and upon hearing my admission rejoined 'you want some of this you yee bastard' (pointing to his split head). Feeling the utmost sympathy for the lad I offered 'Don't you think I'd rather I had that than you?' to which he replied 'Well you know where the bastard is, don't you?' implying that nothing was stopping me going on those lines if I really wanted.

Later, initiatives were kept secret, approval was asked from no-one until we were eventually co-ordinated into a central operation.

From Ollerton the phone messages started to come through of major violence, reinforcements requested. Frickley reported all its buses turned back on way to Ollerton. Hatfield reports arrests and hospitalisations. Phone messages to all miners' welfares converge on Ollerton top priority.

1.40 pm Hatfield reports picket killed, hit in throat by brick, inform all area officials and national officials, request 'flood Ollerton'.

3.10 am Jack Taylor informs all centres they are on way to Ollerton, overrides all instructions to deploy pickets to Ollerton, go to previous targets.

4.35 am Entry reads, Arthur Scargill involved, Ollerton is closed, two minutes silence observed, all pickets to be dispersed, deploy pickets to other pits.

4.55 am Area Agent request to centre, 'we try and get pickets to cool it.'

5.25 am Area legal office requests names and addresses of all lads at Ollerton who witnessed incident.

6.15 am Area HQ requesting assistance at Thoresby where pickets are hard pressed.

7.16 am Hatfield phones to report Crusczczak, one of their pickets, badly beaten, admitted to Mansfield hospital.

7.20 am Askern reports SPG now in operation at Bilsthorpe 'putting boot in.' Arrests.

7.30 am Donny pickets to Thoresby.

8.25 am Clipstone, only six men went to work off the whole day shift.

10.30 am Report from Barnsley HQ SPG units converging on Nottingham from all over Britain, maximum build up this afternoon, Nottingham balloting on strike or not.

Reports of arrests all over coalfield.

The Panels

As soon as the strike was confirmed an emergency meeting of the panels took place, this in order to get picket operations on the road. The panels each elected a picket co-ordinator and a team of men who would man the panel area strike HQ to co-ordinate with Barnsley, to check coal dockets (coal was to be allowed to hospitals, old folk homes and to persons referred to us as in special need by the DHSS. These we would allow an amount of fuel, if delivered by non scab drivers who we cleared day to day at the various strike HQs.) Doncaster strike HQ was to be as in previous years, the Home Coal Garage at Brodsworth, or rather the office of the garage.

At branch meetings throughout the coalfield pickets had volunteered for duty. At each panel HQ the branches presented the numbers of their volunteers and numbers of cars at their disposal. The uneven strengths of political and class consciousness in the respective panels, the differing traditions between constitutionalism and direct action together with the differing degree of 'head' which was given by area leaderships, ensured that the response to the call for pickets would vary. Doncaster, true to its militant traditions, provided almost half of all the Yorkshire pickets even though it numbered no more than a quarter of the total membership. This fact was to cause great problems within the structure of the union as the weight came on and differing sections pulled for greater resources.

It was also a fact that once the Area HQs had been established local area leaders had different ideas on tactics and responses to the situation. They ranged from 'wet' and 'low key' to civil disobedience and direct action. As the scale of the police response to the pickets went off the dial, so the dynamism and confrontational counter-force of the Doncaster pickets started to win the admiration of rank and filers from other panels, who soon found every pretence they could for joining up with the Doncaster direction. This process culminated in the great motorway blockade, which not only caught the country's imagination and the police's breath, it led the South Yorkshire panel leadership to seek a merger of our forces so as to join with our initiatives. When this

25

happened alarm bells started ringing in Barnsley, and somebody whispered into somebody's ear that the total direction of most of the Yorkshire pickets could soon be in the hands of the Doncaster HQ. At this crucial point, the area direction teams were stood down, the local autonomy of picket direction was dissolved and a central co-ordinating committee was to take charge of all pickets in Yorkshire.

The transfer of authority to Barnsley wasn't a total bureaucratic coup by any stretch of the imagination (although the decision to transfer the authority clearly came from the area officials for entirely bureaucratic reasons). It was not to be the four officials dictating when and where and how, indeed the area officials as such kept strictly out of the control and planning of picketing.

If the intention had been to throw off Doncaster's militant direction it only partially succeeded. For one, the area co-ordinator was now appointed onto the area committee along with the area agent, and although this now meant more or less open declaration of targets and strategy with the subsequent right of veto by the other areas, it sometimes, on occasion, went the other way. Doncaster's planners were to have fierce arguments with the committee, with the other planners often drawing back in shock at the scale or the illegality or the possible legal repercussions from the plan. But overall the picket offensive was kept on the road, throughout all the months of mass pressure to stand them down or call them off. Moderate and militant alike shook off the pressure from all sides, and the Yorkshire pickets carried forward the major weight of the strike on the streets.

A lot of the planning was left rather open to allow for the initiative of the picket on the ground. The old panel HQs were thus able to draw in the detail themselves and adapt the plan more or less to their local tradition in one sense or the other. The extracts which follow come from notes made on the Doncaster HQ picket log and at the time, being often short, one paragraph notes, they only give the very broadest outline sketch of the events as they unfolded. They are very useful however in keeping the chronology of what happened, the booms and slumps of the operation, and above all show in the early months of the strike that the pickets did enjoy considerable success in Nottingham whenever they were allowed to picket and show their determination. It was only as the police determined that Nottingham men would work, and picketing would stop that the waverers lost their excuse not to cross the line and went to work.

Ian MacGregor in his big colouring-in book *The Enemies Within* is quite revealing on the subject and success of the pickets. He describes most of the pickets as being 'young and from the Doncaster coalfield' as if those facts were two features which explain their presence on the lines, he also states quite clearly that whenever the pickets were in position the bulk of Nottingham and Leicester pits didn't work, the colliers from those mines would turn up, see the picket and go home, presumably that kept them right with the boss and the missus and didn't upset the bulk of the NUM either. Willing or not, by and large without violence, but with a show of determination, the southern coalfields didn't work. Mac tells how he flew into a rage at the success of these pickets, and how he hot tailed it down to Downing Street to tell Maggie that the British cops were too soft - they weren't stopping the pickets picketing. He even suggested calling over some 'real red neck US sheriffs' who he had called in to sort out our American brothers, to get tough with us. There was no need however, Maggie had the message and some real red neck British cops were drafted in to break the picket lines, stop the pickets no matter how peaceful from picketing, stop them arriving or setting off, and make a big point of getting the reluctant Notts men who up until this time had been simple fence sitters, into strike breakers. Around this time the propaganda 'Back to Work' wagon was cranked up and the press fell into line making reluctant non workers first into reluctant scabs and then lo and behold into National Heroes.

With the orders coming direct from No 10 as to the style of the operation the police should use, the thug tactics went into gear. The purpose was terrorism in the real sense of the word. They would go in hard enough to do some real damage, smash skulls, break bones, render unconscious or kill if it came to that. The object was to terrorise the young (and some old) pickets never to come back again. In the darkness away from the TV camera, to show the iron fist of the state to the young unprotected flesh of the miners. Many did in fact stop picketing after the first few weeks of naked violence. Some are terrified to this day by the nearest thing to a murderer trying to kill them they have or will ever encounter. The plan, under the immunity of police protection and a silenced media, worked with many, but not all by any means. It was in these first sickening days of police terror tactics that the layers of respect for the police which many of the older men had built up all their lives started to peel away. It was then that many a young man tended a fire in his soul of all consuming hatred, and stifled desire to retaliate. . . .until the time came, or flesh and blood could stand no more.

The Struggle Within

One gets only the merest indication of the struggle within the union's structure over picketing, directions, control and size, but the struggle there was at times verging on the most bitter accusations.

As the weight of the whole state machine came upon the union in Yorkshire so the various departmental allegiances vied with each other for retention of funds, for placing this priority above that one, to limit one corner of the operation in order to maximise the other. Those waves broke hardest at the door of finance, and the Financial Secretary, whose objective throughout was safeguarding the funds, found himself, at least in the opening months of the strike, at odds with those local leaders who wished to pull out all stops and flood the country with pickets. At one time under his influence the number of pickets was strictly stipulated to no more than seven cars per branch. At a time when enthusiasm was highest this acted as a bucket of cold water and many who were keen to picket in the early days ended up doing odd jobs for themselves instead. Whilst the great number of volunteers crushing forward for action was greeted by the Doncaster leadership with pride, the finance department regarded it as 'people jumping on the bandwagon'. As Doncaster's bill for petrol escalated far and away above the other Yorkshire areas, the local leaders pointed to numbers of men in the field, while the finance department saw it as a sign 'we were being pillocked'. The complaints over money got to such a point that the whole of the Doncaster pickets were on the verge of being stood down in protest. While public arguments rang across the HQ floor, telephones screamed out demands for pickets and assistance. Eventually at the intervention of other sections of the area leadership, probably Sammy Thompson, the pickets were given more or less their head in terms of everyone being given a place who wanted one. Whilst this was true of Doncaster, throughout the strike almost until the end, pickets from elsewhere, notably North Yorkshire, complained that they were not being deployed and no attempt was being made to recruit large numbers of pickets.

These short notes then will serve as a reminder of all those conflicts and pressures as the union slowly turned broadside to meet the biggest offensive yet mounted to destroy a cornerstone of the whole labour movement.

Extract from Picket Log

The story of the Hatfield/Armthorpe team is one they will tell to their grandchildren, enough to say that their specialist dynamism was such that 'crack' police thugs were deployed to Nottingham to match them, track them and stay with them. Injuries were building up and arrests were disproportionate to other lodge casualties. For this reason a move was made to shift these units to another coalfield. So it was that the joint Hatfield/Armthorpe detachment shifted to Coventry. They arrived to a token force of police numbering not more than 12 'bobbies'. The ballot on strike action had not yet been taken. The men talked to committee men, introduced themselves around the village, explained the case, played a soft key. Looked up all ex-transferee (from Geordieland and Scotland) mates, spread the word by persuasion.

Soon the strike centre was recording that Coventry Colliery was closed. Agreed that safety men work on a heating, no aggro, man to man discussion, Coventry is down.

Pickets staying with Coventry miners' families, requests to arrange something about payment of picket money, etc.

Ellistown, pit turned back, no problem.

Whitwick turned back by Hickie, no problems.

Hickie team at Coalville, nights turned back, no problem.

Daw Mill, night shift returned home, no assistance required.

1.45 am Cadley Hill pit on strike.

16th March 84
Coventry Colliery

The police have by now realised that two of the Donny crack units are in operation elsewhere than Notts. Big shifts in police deployment take place. Coventry suddenly experiences massive police presence.

Armthorpe reports, they and Hatfield together with a large Coventry picket stand the day shift solid, despite intimidation.

7.20 am Frickley report that Ellistown men and all of NACODS have gone back, the pit is idle.

Rossington report 55% Bagworth men gone back, (250 in total working).

Hickie report Baddesley men all turned back.

Brodsworth, all Daw Mill turned back.

Edlington, South Leicester, very few crossed the line.

9.05 pm Hickie, Lea Hall afternoon shift gone back, pickets staying over to stop night shift.

11.15 pm Report very good picket, Lea Hall turned back, pickets returning home.

19th March 84

3.20 pm Edlington, Hickleton, Frickley, Hatfield, Askern, Armthorpe, on their way to Harworth.

4.40 pm Edlington establish small picket on Harworth gates, couldn't phone in, all public phone boxes cut off. Strong police presence.

5.25 pm Police only allow 6 pickets on gate.

6.45 pm Hickleton men report back, 300 police in operation at Harworth.

7.38 pm Armthorpe, back from Bevercotes, report police preventing picketing, wouldn't allow them or the Bevercotes men to picket or talk to others.

Deployment as of 19th March 84

HARWORTH - Days, afters, nights. 7 cars per shift, Edlington, Frickley,

Hickleton.

BEVERCOTES - ditto, Askern, Hatfield.

THORSBY - ditto, Bentley, Rossington, Brodsworth.

BILSTHORPE - ditto.

GOLDTHORPE - Winders will try and help. Armthorpe, Carcroft will filter through when they can.

10.15 am A number of Askern pickets lobby the centre in support of the idea that all Doncaster pickets should take one Nottingham pit at a time. Explain that it is the decision of the panel to try and conform to the EC instruction to try and stop all Nottingham pits with numbers restricted to 7 cars per branch.

12.35 pm Brodsworth, Afters pickets report that Thorsby men bundled through the lines and went to work. Pickets transferred to Ollerton, but got the same reaction. Suggested either stop there for the night shift or make way to Barnsley offices blockade to resist receivers.

12.55 pm Phil Jones of Goldthorpe reports his men at Bilsthorpe did 4 hour picket, police told them to leave county immediately or face arrest.

Tried to establish contact with Nottingham ASLEF to prevent wagons getting in or out of Nottingham. No success as yet.

1.45 pm Hatfield report, they got through but police are preventing them picketing in any fashion.

3.05 pm News received that the area around Barnsley offices is blockaded completely, closing off the building. The news is that the court, on request from the Board, have adjourned the case.

6.00 pm Armthorpe phoned in, Coventry colliery stood.

Made contact with ASLEF Notts and obtained from them the number of the General Secretary of the Notts Area ALSEF with a hope of getting them to black the wagons to Nottingham.

8.15 pm Armthorpe reports, Harworth night shift has been withdrawn as there are not enough men to work it, and not enough police to cover it, nights will be transferred into afters.

9.25 pm Message from Barnsley, barge unloading at Grove Wharf. Armthorpe getting 2 cars away, Hatfield 2 cars away.

9.55 pm Bilsthorpe, pickets not allowed to talk to men going through.

11.30 pm Pickets at Grove Wharf, bobbies present.

12.10 and 12.44 am Reports from Yorkshire Main pickets from Thorsby and Bevercotes, police wouldn't allow contact with workforce.

20th March

4.15 am Grove Wharf, Armthorpe report Spanish ship full of anthracite. Help required, divert any spare men to Grove Wharf. Scab labour transporting fuel.

4.30 am Report of police surveillance of men on Scunthorpe Road (Grove Wharf).

5.00 am Hickleton at Harworth, report 50 dogs in the field.
5.09 am Bentley and Askern lads turned back, threatened with arrest at Blyth roundabout.

8.19 am Bilsthorpe, Goldthorpe, report they cannot talk to anyone, police intervening. Day shift working. Pickets on way home.

9.15 am Spoke to Ray Buckton (D. D.) about problem of wagons. The idea of picketing the depots doesn't work because the BR Board would send all railwaymen home and not just those involved in blacking coal wagons. We are to consider sticking pickets on inward yards/freight yards where the empty wagons leave from or the full ones are stored. Working out way to get pickets to correct place to starve Notts of wagons. Buckton to check and call back.

9.45 am Hickleton reports pickets' cars being photographed coming off A1 (M) by police.

32

10.00 am COSA people again complained that nobody was picketing Coal House and some COSA strikers are becoming disillusioned that we didn't seem bothered either. Sent car from Broddy to put pickets on.

AV Harris Reed lorries running through picket lines at Grove Wharf, contact Dockers' union.

COSA clerks phoned looking for David Murdoch. It transpires that nobody is picketing Coal House. Also it seems that Coal House prepares the wages for Nottinghamshre. This work is normally done by the COSA clerks who are on strike. Argument is that if they can't get APEX to strike at least they should stop doing COSA work. This is obviously of immense strategic importance. Contacted APEX in Bradford, had ridiculous conversation with people on the other end, told to submit the question in writing to Mr Hayworth.

(Longer extracts from the picket log are on computer disc at the Kate Sharpley Library, BM Hurricane, London WC1N 3XX.)

The Strike Co-ordinating Committee

The first meeting of this committee glistened with top brass and an air of 'right, now we're running this show, this is how it's done.' The committee claimed membership by the area officials, the area agents and one lay EC member from each of the Yorkshire areas. By the 13th April the four area officials were no longer directing the committee (owing to other pressures and demands nationwide), although it was customary for one of them to chair the meeting.

The committee began by stating its priorities:
1 Prevent the movement of coal (to and from power stations, depots, etc.).
2 To picket collieries continuing to work.

Because of the heavy police harassment of the Doncaster pickets and the many road blocks on the Doncaster approach roads, the local HQ had been concentrating on wharves etc., and this continued together with the area power stations. There was a continuing problem with pickets at power stations. In Yorkshire we received total co-operation, so there was little to do and little going on. There was a temptation therefore to nick off to the local pub instead of manning the watch 24 hours a day as instructed. It became the devil's own game keeping people on these thankless positions. Although as the bail conditions banned more and more people from Notts and the wharves it became the only place left for some men to go on duty.

By the 4th April we started to encounter trouble from 'leftist' groups who thought they knew best the places to mount pickets. From time to time they completely negated a well thought out plan, by reducing our numbers in strategic areas. Because they didn't know the total operation, they concluded that the small part of it which was visible was useless and therefore should be ignored. Often the plan of the leftist group was no more than a spur of the moment idea which sounded militant at the time but either led to mass arrests, by leading people into a trap we ourselves had avoided, or else it was a damp squid with no co-ordination. The committee decided to take a strong stand on the issue.

It was agreed that pickets should stick to the targets designated by the strike committee and not to go to targets such as NCB offices. It was agreed that anyone picketing at places other than those designated by the committee would not receive expenses or legal representation. It was stressed that more discipline was needed amongst pickets. Notices to this effect were to be placed at Strike Centre.
(Strike Co-ordinating Committee, 4th April 84)

Doncaster targets 4th April.
Drax and Thorpe Marsh power stations.
Gunness, Barton on Humber, Grove, Howden, and Foster wharves.
Harworth and Rufford collieries.

They were later to report that the wharves were 'in hand,' that Harworth had stopped work but that Rufford was not a success.

The Doncaster Area Panel meeting had made one or two comments concerning recent decisions of this Co-ordinating Committee, the first concerning arrests of members not picketing where they have been sent to, the second being the picketing of Coal House and Grimethorpe, and the third being about demonstrations and rallies being held on the 14th April. It was agreed that on one, the matter could be brought up before the next EC. On item two it was said we could arrange picketing at these places of work periodically, but only with the consent of the committee, and that three, Mr O Briscoe and Sammy Thompson and the North Yorkshire and Doncaster area branches attend the rally to be held in Doncaster on the 14th April 1984 and that Mr J Taylor and Mr K Holmer and the Barnsley and South Yorkshire branches attend the rally in Chesterfield on 14th April 1984. Branches ought to be advised to bring banners but bands were only to be engaged with official consent. (SCC, 5th April)

It was further agreed that a push be made in Nottingham in view of the advice given to that area by Messrs Chadburn and Richardson, not to cross picket lines. Each area was to choose a colliery and a fall back to be picketed on Monday's Days and Afters shifts. (SCC, 13th April)

Doncaster reported a first class turnout although there was worry that if picketing and demonstrations clashed picketing would collapse.

It was agreed that in future we do not organise three demonstrations in the same day.

Fines. Doncaster complained that asking pickets not to picket after being arrested meant running short of pickets. Agreed to put the whole matter before the EC.

25th April

Whereas the previous tussle for control of the pickets had been between the local command centres against the Barnsley Yorkshire Area HQ, now we saw signs of a struggle between the national office and the Area. The latter in setting up the co-ordinating committee had taken the reins of its own troops. But to what extent were these troops the national office's? It was clear that no direct link or command ran from Arthur's office through the coalfields, although the press from start to finish tried to maintain he was the godfather running the show.

Weeks after the start of the strike the NEC set up what it called the National Strike Co-ordinating Centre, and manned it up, ironically with one of the Yorkshire NEC members. This seemed fair enough from an information and perhaps co-ordination angle. The trouble came when the national office felt it suddenly had the power to direct the Yorkshire pickets where it felt best. Reminiscent of the old 'no taxation without representation' demand, the area office replied that since National wasn't paying the pickets, didn't meet the costs of the petrol or the legal expenses or the accommodation etc., it couldn't expect to deploy them.

Later in the strike Arthur seemed to go over the head of the area command and call for pickets to Orgreave or Mansfield. This had the effect of completely nullifying the orders and targets of the area HQ as the pickets immediately fell into line with Arthur's public call.

Mr Taylor said he had had words with National Office and they had no authority whatsoever over this committee to agree or disagree to send pickets as they think necessary.

During the night and early hours requests have been received from National Office for our pickets to relieve COSA who had been on duty there the previous day. The strike centre had deployed pickets and referred the matter to this committee. It was decided that this committee deploy pickets and that any request from National Office or any other area be discussed. National Office were informed that they were not to request the deployment of pickets. A notice was produced to that effect for display in Area Strike Centres.
(SCC, 27th April)

....a circular to be sent to all Branches informing them that 60% of Notts miners were now on strike. Notts area were contacted and it was agreed that a letter signed by their officials be forwarded to us containing that information.

Dispensations

This had been an attempt to neutralise some of the opposition, and not to take too callous a line toward other struggling industries. Some processes like Coalite charged that the ovens couldn't go cold or the grates would cool and crack and the whole works would be finished with the consequential loss in demand for coal used by that industry. We had to try and achieve a level of production which allowed the process to continue, but not profit. In addition we demanded that all the Coalite produced could only go to places which we deemed essential - hospitals, schools, sickness cases, etc. These were given a docket, stamped by our local strike HQs. In addition we dictated who delivered that fuel. Any driver or firm who crossed our picket lines would not be allowed to work on these Coalite projects. Again the driver and his firm would have to apply to the local strike HQ for vetting, and a docket stamped by the NUM to say he was OK. He would then stick a sign in his front cab window saying 'NUM Approved Load' and know that he didn't risk assault or blacking.

The question of the steel works was, however, difficult. They had informed us of a similar requirement. The ovens needed fuel, iron had to be produced to keep the process running. How much fuel? In return we had demanded that no steel arches for the Notts pits be supplied and these stopped on April 19th. Some control was exerted. At the same time, the decision caused furious argument. Arthur was publicly saying that no dispensations should be taking place.

Certain of the leftist groups were saying that no coal was supplied when the steel workers had their strike in 81 and the ovens weren't affected. There was an air of deception and a feeling that despite the regular site inspections by Sammy Thompson at the BSC Scunthorpe that we were being pillocked. But this was not yet the Committee's view.

It was agreed that the whole area of dispensations ought to be put forward to the meeting of Area and National officials due to take place today, as there was a danger that the refusal of dispensations could endanger the support we had received from other unions.
(SCC, Barnsley, 30th April)

As it turned out the national meeting broke up in argument. The Yorkshire representatives walked out after taking criticism from Jack Collins, the fiery Kent leader. Neither Scotland nor Wales were represented at the meeting.

Sammy Thompson reported to the meeting that he had visited the Scunthorpe Steelworks along with Branch Officials of the appropriate unions to determine the level of coal stocks as reports had been received of loads of coal being delivered. After an exhaustive visit Mr Thompson and Mr Clark had ascertained that Scunthorpe had no coal at all other than delivered from Yorkshire under dispensation. Indeed Mr Thompson had been informed that Scunthorpe Steelworks was losing £1.5 million a week.
(SCC, Barnsley, 2nd May)

Men on strike in Notts 8th May

Harworth	150	Clipstone	500
Cresswell	450	Sherwood	500
Bevercotes	500	Blidworth	650
Ollerton	500	Rufford	650
Silverhill	76	Pye Hill	40
Welbeck	600	Bentinck	30
Thoresby	650	Calverton working normally	
Sutton	100	Hucknall don't know	
Mansfield	300	Linby	450

38

Annesle	100	Gedling	150
Babbington			
working normally			
Newstead			
over 50% on strike			
Cotgrave	don't know		

Agreed that we choose Cresswell colliery for our target with pickets going to any surrounding pits as a fallback. It was agreed to picket the afternoon shift arriving at 11 am and to stay in position for the day shift coming out. It was also agreed to take some propaganda so that this can be distributed in the area after the picketing had finished.
(SCC, Barnsley, 8th May)

Doncaster area - Silverhill to create a diversion and commencing at 10 am. With the other three areas going to Bevercotes colliery from 11 am. It is about time each panel instructs members who are going on picket lines where to stand and not to be automatically shepherded behind police lines.
(SCC, Barnsley, 9th May)

Subsequent report was that the diversion tactic had been very successful, being the more southern colliery, the police were drawn from the northern area opening it up for the later, bigger picket.

The Plan for Silverhill

Was quite ingenious. The pickets would take small and obscure roads using cars, vans and/or buses, preferably under cover of darkness. Before getting to the road blocks which we had (prior to the operation) reconnoitred, we would drop all the pickets on the hard shoulder at the first overhead bridge past junction 29, so they can get to the overhead road by walking, and assemble at Hardwick Hall car park then walk the one mile to Silverhill Colliery, and launch a mass picket by surprise. The vehicles of course carried on, with only the driver, clean past the road blocks without detection, these were spread out until pick up points were reached after the operation.

The plan, in its sealed envelope, was handed over the night before in the strike HQ at Doncaster, a signature across the seal, not to be opened until the morning when the plan is read to the departing pickets. Secrecy was the essence to defeat police surveillance and infiltration into the local pubs etc.

11th May

The number of pickets suffering head injuries due to police using truncheons is increasing, and therefore it is felt that a cost exercise should be done in obtaining some helmets. It was left for David Douglass to check on the cost of some form of protective head gear.

A letter had been received from JH Thompson concerning a meeting he had attended at the Doncaster Trades Council which was suggesting that we picket Coal House - it was decided to contact Dave Murdoch to ask him to do this. . . .

Coal House, the NCB HQ, was another flash point between the Barnsley HQ and the Doncaster pickets. The latter were incensed by this massive bastion of relative comfort, working away day in day out while we struck. The people from the office walking, laughing through the small group of pickets, while families shivered before empty grates. There was never any love lost between Coal House and the miners when we were at work. Now we were on strike, it was like having salt rubbed daily into a wound. The Doncaster pickets pressed to go to Coal House. The area leaders, particularly Briscoe, were determined that we should not. Just why was never plain, perhaps because the scenes inevitably led to violence and the charge of 'big bully miners threatening small innocent girls' was one that didn't fit into the miner's sense of himself. Because the HQ was built right next door to the Doncaster police headquarters, and they always turn out in force. Perhaps because our attempts to shut it in 72 failed amid some of the worst scenes of violence in the strike, and the worst coverage by the press imaginable. For any or all of these reasons they didn't want us to go. Our earlier 'goes' at shutting it, under the Doncaster leadership, had not been successful and the police had waded in with snatch squads and dogs. The big plate glass windows had taken some of the pickets' frustrations, but apart from that, apart from the bitterness felt against the scabs, who included women, the pickets couldn't bring themselves to confront women in anything like the way they would confront males doing the same job and crossing lines. Also some female pickets were wives and daughters of Doncaster striking miners.

40

Helmets

After long discussion on this matter the report which had been prepared by David Douglass was noted! (ie pickets would not be issued with helmets, contrary to Dave's recommendation)

The Wharves

After months of trying to get a mass picket on the wharves to stop that arterial flood, Doncaster got permission for an all out effort. Unfortunately other forces had intervened and redirected the pickets elsewhere. The *Socialist Worker* of that morning carried an instruction about all going to Scunthorpe. Some of the wharf pickets ended up there, as did some of South Yorkshire's who were sent to Thoresby, the finger seemed to point at the SWP who had the very worst record for substitutionism in the strike, and a hatred for the co-ordinating committee which verged on the paranoid.

David Douglass had arranged for the Doncaster Area to picket wharves but at 7 am nobody turned up because someone had gone along to the members after they had been told where to go and redirected them to Coal House. He was trying to track down who had redirected the men. It was said by Mr Cave that the people concerned would be told in no uncertain terms at tomorrow's panel meeting that they must go where they are sent by members of this co-ordinating committee. The Socialist Workers Party had set up a fighting fund but none of this money was coming back to the NUM. It was decided after a very long discussion that on this occasion to pay the pickets, but in future unless members of this co-ordinating committee direct men where to picket then no payment will be made. It was suggested that a public statement concerning the Socialist Workers Party and what it was trying to do should be distributed. A circular could go out to all Branches telling them that money is not coming into the NUM.
(SCC, 22nd May)

Orgreave

Somewhere in the middle of all the deployments and discussion the agreement with BSC broke down. They were not prepared to consider our stand should concern them. They determined they would fuel themselves without our acknowledgment or agreement. The gauntlet

41

was thrown down in our own back yard and because it was our own back yard, in the heart of Yorkshire, like Coal House it was to twist the tiger's tail. Doncaster's strategy, and subsequently the area co-ordinating committee strategy, was based on flexible targeting. We recognised that Yorkshire at best had something like 5,500 pickets. The police could call on 18,000, they had the latest computers and tracking devices, we had pit wit, pit sense, our skill in surviving. We knew that we could not take head on battles, and sustain them for any length of time. We were an army right enough, but a guerilla army, an army which must act in all the traditional skills of a guerilla army. Surprise had to be the key. Doing the unexpected, making the enemy believe we were in one place, when we would turn up at another. Our success in doing this had made the police look silly and outflanked by our resourcefulness, it made much of the public sit up and respect our resilience. The press called it a 'cat and mouse game.' It had been, but we had never been the mouse! With the advent of Orgreave as a target an immediate split on strategy occurred. Arthur and much of the left saw this as the Saltley Gate turning point of the strike. A static target to concentrate on, win a colossal victory, and turn the tide of the strike. We disagreed. We thought Orgreave today, but tomorrow, let them go to Orgreave ù we'll be in Notts or at the wharves, let Orgreave be one target, not the target. It was not to be. While it stayed open it deflected the central thrust of our strategy. The police for their part were highly delighted to have the troublesome miners all in one place at one time. They knew where we would be, they set out their troops like Sitting Bull prepared for Custer, then they brayed us to hell.

Ian MacGregor's book, *The Enemies Within*, gloats with satisfaction on the turn to Orgreave and even suggests that it was a totally unnecessary exercise on our behalf. It had the effect of drawing all our pickets out of Notts. Mac says, it allowed the Notts pits to go back into production. It broke the continuation of daily picketing in that coalfield and allowed Notts men who hadn't previously gone to work, to go to work. He also tells us that while we battled it out at Orgreave the coal was pouring in through Flixborough wharf quite unhindered, and that adequate supplies of coke were got straight in through BSC's own wharf, all of which made Orgreave's fuel unnecessary.

Tactically it was a mistake, but at first the pickets thought it was the government's Waterloo and dynamically flung themselves into the fray.

42

Once Orgreave had arrived, and once the injuries started, two things happened. One, the National President made very public and very clear that this was where he wanted the pickets to go. Having had that word of command from the man they would follow to the end of the earth, there was little we could do to stop them. Second, as the injuries built up a 'right you bastards' syndrome built up, with men eager for revenge, bottling up their hate for the next go and the next go and the next. Pure heroism and rage stripped to the skin threw itself at the robotoid lines of armoured men. In addition the SWP, Workers Power, et al., made Orgreave the test of a true socialist. If you didn't think Orgreave was right you were an agent, a spy and a traitor. They contrasted Orgreave, with Scargill and the pickets, to Taylor, Kinnock and a weak line towards picketing. It had never been that way. The strategy for a guerilla response was a strong mass picket strategy, the concentration on Orgreave became a sort of First World War swamp in which our forces got bogged down in the blood and battle. The paper sellers never fought there themselves, of course, they only talked about it.

Meeting with National President

Mr Homer reported on yesterday's meeting between our Area Officials and Mr A Scargill at which Mr Scargill has suggested that Orgreave coking plant should be picketed every day. An opinion was expressed as to first of all picketing on day shift at Notts and then going to Orgreave or vice-versa. It was felt that we could not let Orgreave go. It was decided therefore to picket Calverton colliery from 5 am in line with the National Co-ordinating Committee request and then fall back to Orgreave.
(SCC, 31st May)

Having got Orgreave as a target, the committee attempted to put some order into the scene and organise the action, splitting the forces between the top gate and the bottom gate, trying to organise collective responses and advances rather than the host of periodic impromptu sorties which, strangely enough, frequently took place after the scab lorries had either got in, or well away with their loads.

Orgreave

A very long discussion took place with regard to the picketing of the Orgreave plant and it was felt that politically we could not withdraw. It was felt therefore the best solution to the problem was to picket Or-

43

greave on an irregular basis rather than every day.

This contrasted of course with Arthur's perspective. He saw this as a singular target, one at which we could nationally muster our forces. Sheffield, like Birmingham in the case of Saltley Gate, was a big industrial centre with a great many strong trade unions. Saltley had become a great rallying point for the whole class during the 72 dispute - it was the touchstone of involvement which signified a possible general strike. Could Orgreave, sitting on the gates of Sheffield, be the same? Would the steel workers, engineers and heavy plant workers march at the side of the miners and so bury the site in a mass outpouring of popular support for the miners and revulsion of scabbing so that the police would be forced to close the gates themselves as they had done at Saltley? We could rally all our national pickets from the four corners of the island and be one union, publicly and visibly engaged in a daily struggle. We could be a focus for all the movement of the left and progressive forces to become involved in this dispute, with a single short perspective - shut the plant! That at least was the alternative perspective.

Continuing our policy of flexibility the committee decided 6th June
Doncaster to Notts and then back to wharves
S Yorks to Notts and then to Orgreave
Barnsley to Notts and then to Houghton (winders working)
N Yorkshire to Lancashire.

Whilst at Orgreave
Token picket keeping masses of police at this plant.
(SCC, 11th June)

Meanwhile, contrary to the leftist charge that we were stopping people volunteering for picketing, by this point in the dispute we were very publicly requesting them.

Sheffield AUEW Confederation 28. Reported support on picket lines offered by rank and file. Regional Officer should be approached to see if this is possible, this matter to be taken up by Gen. Sec. with union officials concerned.

Suggestion of a leaflet be produced for the demonstration imploring our members to join picket lines in support of the NUM.

The Sheffield steel workers, who were looking to get whole branches to march to our side, take one day strike or just be daily on the line with us, had been met by much the same kind of obstruction we were to face in 86 when miners tried to get on printers picket lines. We were told that an 'official request would have to come from the union officials, as we don't want to interfere.' Getting the Official Request is of course the devil's own job, and if it's ambiguously worded it gets the official off the peg, all of which delays efforts to get solidarity action when the iron is hot.

Poland

It has taken some time to get the embassy picketed, but on Wednesday June 20th Doncaster pickets were delegated to do it. The national office had had it for some time, had passed it on to Kent, but for one reason or another, some say the Kent leadership being 'soft' on the Polish government, it hadn't happened. Even when the Doncaster (Hatfield) pickets arrived it was a day or two before they got themselves into position and many thought they too were being seduced away from the embassy, although they deny it. When they got in position it wasn't long before the comrades at the embassy sent for the diplomatic (armed) police who were none too gentlemanly in removing the pickets and their posters. Arrest was to be instantaneous, so it was felt there was no point trying to continue. In about a week the pickets withdrew.

The Humber Bridge

The blockade of the Humber Bridge was of course directly inspired by the Doncaster picket tactic earlier in the strike of blockading the motorway. The Humber Bridge was a further stage up in the strategy. Whereas the motorway was leading to Notts, the Humber Bridge was not in itself on-route to anywhere. The simple fact was, that by this stage of the strike, the police had all but closed up every trade union right we thought we had enjoyed. We literally were not going to be allowed to picket, in any strength no matter how small or peaceful. The direction of our pickets into Notts, although skilfully outmanoeuvring the police on many occasions, was more or less blocked. The placing of pickets in residence to be domiciled in Notts, and therefore not needing to run the blockade gauntlet, had been placed in serious jeopardy by police attacks upon Notts houses or institutions housing pickets from elsewhere.

Fund raisers were attacked all over the country, the DHSS was tightening every nut on the meagre allowances they give to our children. The courts were finding all pickets guilty unless proven innocent. Offences which didn't exist were being invented; minor offences were given custodial sentences, and pickets were frequently jailed without the right to bail, before being found guilty of anything. Where we made a physical stand the police reacted with outright unrestrained violence and hatred. Conventional picketing, such as was characterised and perfected by the 72 strike was not applicable to the current situation. This was becoming, indeed had become, far more than an industrial relations dispute. This was class war. This was a struggle for different sets of values and a different way of life. We had become a civil resistance movement and it was to civil disobedience that we increasingly had to turn. Such actions as the Humber Bridge, more of a protest or a demonstration at the whole situation the miners were in, were immensely popular with the pickets, almost always they were carried out with the very lightest of spirits and pit humour. They completely routed the police on these occasions and brought grudging tones of critical congratulations from the media for their 'cunning' or 'ingenuity'.

Hit Squads

Were ghosts. The police tried in vain to track them down, but they melted away. The reason was that as organisations or standing teams, they rarely existed. By the first six months of the strike, it was more than obvious we were taking on the whole state machine, that the object was to destroy this union of ours and decimate the industry. The police had declared total war on anyone who dared venture on to the streets to demonstrate or picket, there were few holds barred when they went in to do a job (see the pamphlet *Come and Wet This Truncheon*). The scabs had, to a large extent, presided over this state of affairs. Their leaders were hand in glove with the Thatcher machine, they were willing co-directors in an attempt to crush the social and political force of the NUM. The strikers did not lose any love on the scabs.

True, the vast majority of miners set out each morning to try and persuade the working miners to join us and come over the lines. They wished to talk, to argue, if necessary to push and shove but no more. Day in, day out of being jeered at, laughed at, and set up for a bashing by the scabs frequently changed that attitude of gentle persuasion to a resolution of 'Right, if you bastards want it that way, that's the way you're going to get it.'

A resolution unspoken but alive was present among a hard core of the Doncaster pickets, namely that we had come to stop coal being produced. Notts was bleeding the strength out of the body of our union. Every nut of coal was trivialising our noble sacrifice. The selfish, greedy working miner who could see no further than the end of a pay slip was taking the food out of our children' mouths, they were stopping the strike biting, they were prolonging it, they were undoing everything, which at immense personal sacrifice we had tried to do. The spontaneous rush at Silverhill was not a preconceived design, it was an outpouring of anger and frustration at being mocked, taunted and provoked by the blacklegs going to work. They misjudged the mood of the men, a mood which swept right on through Silverhill and way on down to Harworth.

The Co-ordinating Committee never sanctioned such actions of course and didn't even know the 'Maguires' had been to Harworth. That lack of information was fatal. The Committee had scheduled Harworth as Doncaster's official target the next morning.

Of course the police were itching for revenge because of the night's previous raid, they couldn't believe their luck as the Doncaster pickets arrived, much against their own judgement, the next morning. The police resolved on revenge which they took in full measure.

Targets could be picked, routes planned but the mood of the pickets once they got there (when and if they got there) was an unknown factor. On occasion they could act explosively, at other times a ton of dynamite wouldn't shift them. One of my arrests took place at Calverton where a huge crowd of pickets sat picnicking on the grass. They outnumbered the police three to one, and yet no-one as much as stood by the colliery gate. The blacklegs leisurely rolled by in cars, and even on bikes. All that was missing was for the pickets to exchange a 'good morning' with the blacklegs. As is my wont, I strode into the pickets without once thinking what the response would be, by either the police or pickets, and started haranguing the sitting crowd, that if they weren't going to picket they should stop at home. I ended with the shout 'let's go,' turned and went as two policemen simply grabbed me and took backwards through the crowd to the mobile lock up. After which peace returned to the scene and the lads got the cards out.

47

After the invasion of the Yorkshire coalfield at the end of August, when the NCB planted a scab at each colliery, the police at the pit heads marked out a corner or street where the pickets would be allowed to stand. Nowhere else would be permitted. The lads at first were shuffled and inched into these corrals, but after a week or two, the pickets started to go and stand there quite of their own initiative. Arriving one morning at Brodsworth we were amazed to see the dozen or so pickets standing dutifully on the designated corner, with not a cop in sight! When we went to stand on the opposite side of the road, the men shouted 'you can't stand there!'

On one of the mass pickets at Gunness, the whole of the Doncaster pickets motored along until about one mile from the wharf, whereupon the police had drawn up a couple of transits on the east side of the road. We had almost taken them by surprise, they weren't quite ready for us. To my fury, the convoy, instead of swerving over the west side of the road and steaming past them, stopped. As two lines of riot police formed up across one road, the road opposite which gave equal access to the wharf was totally open. The pickets lined up to face the police ranks, ignoring the open road opposite. In an attempt to get the pickets over that side I set off on my own down the open road, past the couple or so bobbies on that side of the road. A charge by the pickets up that side would have taken them right to the wharf, but that is not the way the pickets wanted to play it for some reason. I was of course arrested. The pickets were as mad with me as I had been with them. They accused me of giving myself up before the going got tough. For my part I couldn't see why chose the path of most resistance, even waiting until the police sent for reinforcements before crashing into the shields. All that was needed was a man with a stop watch and a flag to start the proceedings at a set time.

Most pickets were entirely and thoroughly peaceful, even boring. Some were mere tokens of resistance, on occasion a spark would light up a colossal explosive mixture which somehow accumulated without warning.

Of course, when the few scabs went into the Doncaster pits, this was a deeply cutting insult to the whole community. Almost without exception the villages exploded in indignation and anger. Pickets had been none too happy with people working in Notts, excuses had been wheeled out for them right through the strike. But men going in at our own pits, this was a far more serious and provocative thing. People took it as a personal shame that someone was scabbing at their pit.

Miners also found that their communities were subject to virtual states of siege, their villages occupied by large numbers of police. Freedom of movement outside their immediate communities was severely restricted, while even within mining towns and villages, striking miners and their families found their ability to move around subject to the control of the police. In addition virtual curfews were imposed by the police with anyone on the streets liable to harassment and arrest. (Gordon 1985, p.165)

As stated, when we started into the strike few expected the patterns of picketing and objectives would be any different from the '70s. We intended to stop the use of coal, because we, the coal miners, were on strike. The scale of the state's offensive against our simple objective, showed to even the most conservative that we were not in a normal battle. The government had called a no holds barred contest, authorising the burning of oil and nuclear energy at an increased cost of £30 million per week. It has to be grasped that the NUM is a small union, with less than 200,000 members. The scale of expenditure against the size of the force they were fighting far, far outweighed anything spent in two world wars or the Malvinas debacle. It was our social ideology and vanguard position in the working class as a whole which they were out to defeat, not just defeat but bury, as a warning to any other who would dare contrast our values against theirs. Since it was a government and not industrial inspired assault, it was clear that we had every justification for widespread civil disobedience against this government, and not necessarily to limit ourselves to industrial targets related to coal. For this reason the motorway and Humber Bridge blockade was entirely justified, since we were stopped from stemming the supply of coal, many pickets resolved instead to 'make them pay' by turning up here and there and everywhere, stretching the police resources, and raising the costs of containing us. The ultimate figure was put at around £5 billion, which is a heavy casualty for the government to carry, whether or not we had the long term satisfaction of shutting Notts pits.

Organising to obstruct the state offensive against the miners rarely reached the 'insurrectionist' proportions which MacGregor claimed it did. For a start the 'riots', such as they were, unlike the picketing and tactical manoeuvres to avoid police, had no central or local organising centre. Had the whole thing been a leftist conspiracy it was poorly planned. For a start, a second front would have been opened up in the black areas, with riots taking place in the inner cities. The state's forces would have been outflanked and fighting on a northern and generally southern front at the same time. However it didn't happen. The reason is obvious to all except the paranoid Colonel Blimps in the Home Office. The inner city riots were unplanned, carried through not by a master-mind laying down orders but the ordinary young people of the areas who had just had the final straw placed upon them, usually by heavy and repressive policing. Similarly the 'Molly Maguire' type raids upon Coal Board property or scab centres had no central planning office, no picket 'army council' directing the raids. Like the inner city riots they were the result of having 'had enough,' of having been pushed too far, or having had the end of a truncheon too many times without the chance to hit back.

Right wing Labour politicians, hundreds of miles from the scene of the action, together with the sensationalist newspaper headlines tried to project the idea that 'The Revolutionaries' had moved in and were organising the violence. Everyone and their dog knew that the so called 'Revolutionary Left' confined its fiery image to dialogue and rarely enough engaged in that even. More generally they skirted the edges of crowds offering tablets of gold but never bricks. They certainly couldn't have thrown any themselves since they would have had to drop the armfuls of papers and that is an expellable offence. The truth is that this generation of revolutionaries unlike the 1960s variety keep a good distance between themselves and confrontation of the physical type and have long since lost the authority whereby they could mobilise save alone organise revolutionary resistance to scabs and police. Your average inner city 'rioter' regarded the 'left' as a bit wet, and it wasn't long before your average mining activist thought the same way.

Only a small section of the British Anarchist movement, with their ideology of direct action, tried to generate feelings of insurgency.

The truth of the matter is that after six months of state 'terror' against the miners and their community, those who wanted to, did, those who didn't feel up to it kept mum, neither waited for the staff car bearing the red flag to arrive and organise the shock troops.

The Area Executive Meetings

Following the widespread initiatives of the local panel picket centres, a Special Executive meeting was called in April. There was a brief appraisal of the strike conduct so far and the initiatives of the officials, such as the production of a leaflet aimed at Nottingham miners, putting our case for support. However, the bulk of the meeting was a concerted effort by Barnsley to establish overall control of the strike. In my opinion it was prompted by the dynamic thrust of the Doncaster pickets, and the way they had become the virtual spearhead of the picket action nationwide. Its ability to put out in excess of 2,000 pickets with 500 cars and vans per day meant that from day one our area was putting a greater demand on the resources of the union than the three other areas put together. The arguments between the Doncaster picket co-ordinator, collecting the area's funds each day and the area finance officer were bitter to say the least, the latter believing the situation was out of control and attempting to regulate the numbers. The argument had broken to the surface at EC meetings before, it was related to the deployment question. With more men on the ground, in the field or other areas, the demands for pickets from other counties could be quickly responded to. At times those immediate demands meant that Barnsley's guide lines were only loosely followed, they would say ignored. Previous orders that we send just two cars each to the 14 pits in Nottingham led to so much frustration that we changed to mass picketing of single collieries.

The different characteristics of the men in the Lancashire coalfield as against those in the Nottingham coalfield meant that certain officials could throw about comments that other areas had got the whole of Lancashire to a standstill with only a quarter of the pickets, while Doncaster had scarcely had a success at a single pit on a single shift.

Against bitter argument by the Doncaster representatives we were then cut down to half the finance, and this in turn meant cutting down the numbers we could deploy to seven cars per branch where previously we had sent two or more times that number. Orders to picket the same number of collieries with an even more reduced number of pickets were, quite frankly, regarded as impractical by the Doncaster strike committee, and ways around it sought.

The line from the top table had not been unanimous and a row developed following which, with considerable efforts by Sammy Thompson as far as one could tell, our funds were eventually restored and the full complement of pickets put on the road again.

From that point until this meeting we had our head, and under the local direction from Doncaster, pickets themselves will be able to assess the strengths and weaknesses of how we made out. The record shows that it was far from without success, especially given the odds of something like six to one against.

We succeeded in closing Coal House - something unachievable in 72 or 74. The subsequent presence of up to 1,000 police, intentionally drawn there to relieve pressure on Nottingham (which it didn't do, since the numbers of police just carried on escalating and appeared unlimited) succeeded frequently in having them standing on their own as we went elsewhere. The tactic of not going to Coal House when the police expected us to, despite the protest from Hickleton that we should fight them day and night, was a popular one, and showed to the Doncaster town folk, passing thousands of police guarding six pickets, that we could call the initiative.

The motorway operation speaks for itself although it was brought out in the course of complaints about the way we handled things that it had not been well thought of in Huddersfield Road. Another criticism was of some of one panel and all of another being deployed from Doncaster under the guise of 'back-up' and 'reinforcements'. For the first week and a half of the strike up to one third of all other areas pickets joined with our men. Just the week before South Yorkshire had followed our motorway action and was making moves for joint ventures.

Many plans were ready in the pipeline, which can't be disclosed as we may need them again. The whole of Doncaster's pickets were ready with their Monday morning deployment when the order came to stand them down and cancel all actions, a big push we were told was on the way and would take precedence over all other plans. It was the first serious shot at displacing independent initiatives.

It was followed by the EC meeting that Monday morning. The financial secretary opening the meeting by saying that this was an exercise to get some discipline into the movement, and to take 'frustrations' out of the movement. The men who had to go to picket centres all over Doncaster at 3 am and tell men they had got up for nothing, they were being held off, knew all about frustrations.

It came as a big shock to discover the opening criticisms were of North Yorkshire who, we were surprised to find, had planned actions of their own and had not reported these plans to the Barnsley HQ (strike centre). They had concentrated all efforts on Cotgrave believing an all Yorkshire operation was underway.

The bulk of the debate consisted of area officials and EC members arguing for greater centralisation and directing all control to Barnsley. People, we were told, 'were doing what they like and going anywhere'.

North Yorkshire's EC said we had all been doing our own little things. Inky Thompson, a man attempting to run the Area strike HQ at Barnsley, told us they were never able to establish at any time what was going on. He and Kevin Hughes charged with co-ordinating action had to wait for the TV or newspapers to tell them who had done what.

Sammy Thompson in talking of some of the concrete frustrations pointed out that ASLEF had specifically requested pickets on Ferrybridge, he had told North Yorkshire to supply them and they, in their wisdom, had not done so. Despite certain ASLEF men who had refused to cross picket lines which weren't there, others had no option but to take in oil and fuel for the station.

The bulk of the EC argued that in future all pickets be directed day by day from Barnsley to targets selected by them. Some of the ideas which then emerged were a bit old hat to us. The introduction of a code, which would be changed every day, we had been doing for a week already.

Henry Daly thinking he saw the green light for even more authoritarian structures started talking about punitive measures for any dissident strike committees taking independent initiatives: 'Limit funds to these areas, limit how far they can go on their own, limit what they can do'.

When it came to specific charges against Doncaster, such as our outright refusal to give information on the phone as to how many pickets have been deployed to where, we of course explained the very good reasons why. But the old wounds started to open up again regarding the money we claim. 'Doncaster won't give information to Barnsley on numbers of cars - but they're never late in coming for money for them. They've had plenty money for those cars already.' (Briscoe, Area General Secretary)

Taylor gave the raison d'être that there had been no initiative from Barnsley and no big plan, because nobody would give numbers of who was available. People had been more concerned with doing what they wanted.

Sammy Thompson gave what we considered was a case in point. A big Preston Labour Movement rally at which Kinnock was speaking. At least two bodies involved with the meeting invited speakers from Yorkshire without the knowledge of the other. One was Davie Miller, a member of the Communist Party, the other on a more official level because of the prestigious nature of the platform, was Sammy Thompson, Vice President of the area. No consultation was attempted by Kellingly or North Yorkshire. The result, given the ambiguous response from Yorkshire, terrified that Davie and not Sammy would end up on the same platform as Kinnock and cause him 'embarrassment', was that the NUM spot was cancelled.

For Doncaster, we argued that we were fearful of a wet blanket being thrown at the pickets. That 5,000 pickets couldn't beat 30,000 police in open war and that we were engaged in a guerilla type campaign in which diversity and decentralisation was a strength. The initiatives should be spread over the area controls. This, however, was far from the common view, and it was undeniably true that closer liaison was a necessity and some big plans can only be developed on a county wide level. In the event the decision of the EC was that all operations and all pickets be directed from Barnsley via the organisational committee. There in fact to be four area agents plus as many Area Officials as are available and the Campaign Committee members, which is one from each panel. 'For the sake of continuity' Frank Cave and Inky Thompson got it accepted that Dave Douglass would fill the position for a couple of days in a transitional period. As it turned out my position on the Committee was to last considerably longer.

54

The Council

Tuesday 19th June

Following our annual gala, Edlington raised a serious complaint about the cynical way the so called Socialist Workers Party had buried the gala in their posters (many of them calling for all out action at Orgreave). Which gave a free and numerous advert for their paper (Socialist Worker headed each poster) together with criticism of the picketing strategy we were pursuing. These posters were just handed out to all and sundry who didn't realise who or what was behind them and just innocently carried them. The whole idea was to create the impression that the SWP had massive support among the miners.

The Edlington delegate pointed out that the wish of our community to identify with the strike and carry posters was being exploited. They proposed that the union ought to produce its own posters and distribute them making it clear that these are official posters.

Of course the wider role of the SWP and other groups intent on disrupting the strike led many delegates to launch attacks upon these groups. The right wing used this as an excuse to wet their knickers talking about 'infiltrators, Communists, Trotskyists, etc.'

This opened the door to an attempt to get the council to criticise pickets using violence, which was blocked hard by Askern. In reply to Henry Daly my own contribution pointed out that when attacked by mechanical, helmeted psychopaths with sticks and big boots I didn't ask the right to defend myself, we claimed that right. I told the council that although I might be built like Gandhi, when a herd of police horses was charging down on you at 35 miles an hour, no way was me and my marras going to sit down in front of them and sing 'we shall overcome.'

One of the problems and another excuse for trying to put the dampers on, was the idiots who threw bricks which came down among our lads. These people needed identifying and sorted out by our own men. If necessary told not to bother coming back on picket lines; or else they should join the police ranks and see what damage they could do from there.

Armthorpe tabled a resolution on arrested members. It called for protection for any member jailed who loses his job as a result. That the union insist he be re-employed when he comes out and that his loss of wages be restored.

Inky Thompson seconded it for the Hickleton branch and Hatfield spoke on it, pointing out that we were talking about lads arrested for actions in support of the strike and nothing else. We have an obligation once we've sent lads into action to defend them if they get nicked. Briscoe in the course of his contribution said he had just received a letter from the NEC advising that nobody is to accept disciplinary action from the Board, to ignore letters, don't go for interviews or take part in correspondence. Inform the area. We are obliged, he said, to fight for their reinstatement. That is obviously if the arrested people have been acting under our guidelines as directed by the NUM.

Several moderate delegates fell over each other in indignation, saying people who attacked police stations at weekends or sabotaged equipment on pit tops were on their own.

Holmer insisted we were here to save pits and people at Rossington and Hickleton who sabotaged them were not acting in the interests of the union. This struck me as strange since just prior to this debate Briscoe had talked with optimism of the pressure being applied on the board by modern underground equipment being threatened with loss at the 30 super pits as the strike wore on and the earth took its toll. It seems that what the eye doesn't see the heart doesn't grieve about.

South Kirkby delegate (nicknamed Cavey's pup, because of his resemblance to the eminent agent) raised the question of people not paying various bills and accumulating debts for which they were then jailed, would the same rule apply?

As it turned out, Armthorpe's resolution as it stood was defeated, but the platform's amendment was accepted saying the matter would be raised on the NEC and reaffirming a previous minute to protect people convicted whilst carrying out instructions of the union.

Special Council Meeting

That in the event of any more interference from local management or group management i.e. sending letters to members, we withdraw from any safety cover that may occur.

This was a problem which had arisen from the malicious interference by the Board in using the responsible attitude of our members, against the strike. This was already Doncaster panel's policy, because of the way in which payments for safety work had been manipulated by the Board.

Ian Ferguson, the Panel chairman, spoke in favour of the resolution. The platform called it 'a policy of sabotage' and said it would throw all the pits into jeopardy, they asked that the resolution be withdrawn. Treeton stuck to their guns and when put to the vote we voted 18 for, with 44 against.

However Armthorpe had a similar resolution calling for the withdrawal of our safety men. It read

This Armthorpe branch of the NUM demand that the rescue service be withdrawn in order to combat the Board's propaganda campaign against this union.

It was seconded by Bentley and Doncaster branches spoke for it. Unfortunately it was opposed by Capstick of Stillingfleet, one of the most articulate delegates in the council. He said it was a life or death struggle and we were flying very close to the edge. To everyone's surprise the Brodsworth delegate got up and opposing panel policy said he couldn't support this resolution, nobody could. Briscoe said that if we withdrew our safety men, BACM would withdraw and this would mean the certain end of a great number of pits. When it came to the vote 9 branches voted for it, the rest against.

17th September - the council seen a bobby dazzler of a resolution.

Coming from Grimethorpe it brought to the surface the murmurings of discontent about the conduct of pickets. Under the title of Picket Lines - Discipline, it said

That this area council condemns the policy of brick throwing on picket lines and insists that an EC member be in attendance on each mass picket in an attempt to keep some form of discipline which could lead to a much more effective picket being maintained.

There were some elements throughout the dispute who just wished somehow the strike would go away. They had built an image of themselves as fine upstanding gentlemen of society, democrats and upholders of the law. As loud supporters of 'Law and Order' and condemners of 'the mob' as the Tories were. They hate the confrontations with the police as they see them as the upholders of a system they themselves believe in. The confrontations seemed to be evidence of a class war they had long ago convinced themselves didn't exist. The confrontations were a living evidence of extra-parliamentary action when they had set their eyes on parliament as the only means of redress for all wrongs.

Grimethorpe's resolution opened the door for the charge of 'the right brigade'. Throwing stones was not a way to picket, too many pickets were being deployed anyway, the picket lines were too numerous. This was what was antagonising the police. An Executive member ought to be there to keep order.

The quite legitimate complaint about the cock-eyed man in the crowd who threw stones which landed on our people was opportunistically used as a sympathy getter by the 'play it all down lobby.'

It was seconded by Kellingly.

The Hatfield delegate opposed it calling it 'the most dangerous resolution to appear in the strike.' It was the most divisive, and would drive a wedge between the pickets and the union leadership. It would lead to the total surrender of mass pickets which in turn would mark the collapse of picketing altogether, we suspected this was actually what some people wanted. The collapse of picketing would mean the collapse of the strike which is what certain other people wanted. In any case the resolution was inaccurate, it talked of A Policy of Brick Throwing. There was no such Policy and never had been. If it was passed it would mean that we agreed there had been a policy of brick throwing but now there wouldn't be. The legal implications were horrendous. Secondly it was hypocritical. Where was any mention of police attacks or the huge proportion of our side who get injured against those numbers of police who have? On the question of the bad shots, the pickets would sort those characters out themselves, we were never certain anyway that they were pickets and not policemen who knew exactly what they were throwing at. The delegate concluded by begging Grimethorpe to withdraw the resolution.

Solid support for that line came from Askern, Bentley, Maltby and Rossington and numerous others from all sides of the council chamber.

The platform found itself on a hook of not being able to approve the resolution nor yet condemn it. They asked Grimethorpe to withdraw it in favour of one which condemned all violence 'not least the violence of the police who are the cause of violent responses by our members. We could have lived with that, but Grimethorpe was having none of it. 'What about bricks?' he asked. Taylor tried to fit it in '...condemns all violence and brick throwing etc.' but it wouldn't work. Given Grimethorpe's determination to see it through the Platform had to recommend a vote against. When put to the vote 14 branches voted for it, the rest against.

For some time the Doncaster branches had debated the fate of our men sacked by the Board and tried, almost willed for some form of pledge that they wouldn't be abandoned. Goldthorpe had long feared that despite all the chest beating, the victimised men could be dumped in a haste to find a settlement. They moved

Imprisonment - Picketing - Jobs

This Area seek a guarantee that NUM members imprisoned for authorised picketing offences, will retain their jobs with the National Coal Board.

If such a guarantee cannot be obtained, then financial recompense be made available from union funds for the member's loss of job.

The platform felt that the first part had been covered by the NEC decision and the second part was premature and ought to be left. On a guarantee on the first part the Goldthorpe delegate withdrew the second part.

The next resolution came from Hatfield, but had already got the prior support of the whole panel. It read

Blockade - Thursday 27th September

This council resolves to bring the struggle for jobs to London on Thursday 27th September 1984 with a mass blockade of the financial centre of Britain.

Before the winding up of the Doncaster picket control, we had had a plan to take the fight right into the centre of London and the stock exchange. It was an idea which was still floating around, and we needed approval for. On the 27th the anarchists, the anti-nuclear protestors, the unemployed and the feminists were staging a 'Stop the City' demonstration, London's misfortune could be just the opportunity we needed to take to the City streets and show that the miners' cause was alive and well. We needed a second front opening up, this would be an ideal opportunity.

The resolution let down the murmuring drawbridge again and across it in fine fettle came the charge of the right brigade. Spluttering like outraged Colonel Blimps about public opinion, the law of the land, etc.

Needless to say the platform was against it, it wasn't picketing, not our sort of thing, etc. When put to the vote the resolution got 15 votes. All Doncaster, and a few others, all the rest were against.

On Wednesday 26th September

The Doncaster panel was outraged by the systematic attempts by BACM to get men to work, phoning people up, sending letters, even calling on isolated individuals who lived in town to get them to return. Armthorpe proposed that in retaliation we picket out the Rescue Brigades men. We knew the Area Executive was against it but the whole panel agreed to meet the Rescue Men at Brodsworth, together with officials of every branch and explain to them what was happening.

On 22nd October along the same lines Frickley proposed to the Council

That this branch calls upon the Area Officials to investigate the procedure to expel BACM from the TUC.

The platform advised that the matter was already in NEC business and would be dealt with accordingly, so the resolution ought to be withdrawn. Which it was. But Frickley's next one wasn't.

That this council meeting rescinds the Special Executive Minute 1 (19) of the 7th March 1984 and that branches be allowed to picket members of the BACM under the jurisdiction of the co-ordinating committee. Proposed by Frickley. Seconded by Maltby.

Henry Daly, outraged and indignant, talked of the extremists, of how 'we were talking of shutting our own pits' and earning more public disapproval. It was vehemently opposed by Ken Holmer and Owen Briscoe. For our part we noted that we weren't going to picket all BACM, only those at collieries where BACM members were making fools of us by openly canvassing for scabs and running around isolated hamlets trying to engineer a return to work. Strangely enough Howard Wadworth the Kellingly delegate announced 'well I'm going to shock everyone and support this resolution' which is what he did, however when put to the vote only the Doncaster branches plus about 5 others voted for it.

The final item that day was the question of the rescue men, and the first of many bitter exchanges on the subject. They had sent in a letter which really took the form of an ultimatum. They said they would be totally on strike or totally at work, but not in between and subject to safety work. They would not be doing safety work as requested.

At the bottom of it wasn't the question of safety or the apparatus which they said needed 24 hour attention, it was a simple fact they wanted full payment strike or no strike, and they were told this in no uncertain terms.

The right wing of course felt the rescue men should go to work, they should all be allowed in every day, needed or not, and be on full payments.

After a row, however, the council reaffirmed that its previous decision would stand, the rescue men would be treated the same as everyone else. . . .no better and no worse. By the time of the Emergency Council Meeting of 2nd November 84 we had asked them to provide safety cover where required on the basis of the £5 we pay to other people doing

61

essential work, underground safety work, and coal washing etc. They rejected it, saying that these others only worked 6 hours whereas they do 18 hours inclusive of standby, and they have to put in 7 days a week. So, accepting their arguments, the area officials had worked all the time out on a pro-rata basis. . . .it came to £50. They rejected this also and demanded all or nothing. The situation was now becoming critical with many pits in a position of inundation, collapse and gas accumulation, with nobody able to relieve the situation since the rescue men were refusing to cover even emergency situations.

With a gun to our heads and many expressions of disgust, the platform recommended we allow the rescue men back on the previous terms. We called for a card vote, resulting in 853 to pay them and 247 against, including most of the Doncaster branches.

At the end of November, the lack of direction or any initiatives to take the strike forward from the national or area leadership, seen a number of attempts by branches to open up new fronts.

General Strike, Darfield Main

This branch believes that the activities of the Tory government and Tory courts in attempting to break the strike and smash the union is a threat to Trade Unionism as we know it in this country. The Tories are attempting to take back the rights our fathers and forefathers have fought for during the last 150 years. We believe the TUC should, without any delays, call and organise the most widespread industrial action to counter this threat from the Tories.

If the TUC is unwilling to take these steps then the NUM must give the lead and call for a one day solidarity general strike for the whole Trade Union movement and must name the date for such a strike. Let us not forget that under the circumstances the NUM should never have had to ask the TUC for support. The TUC should not need prompting as the whole Trade Union Movement is under threat.

Just a few days before, the Northumbrian Area had proposed to the NEC the calling for a two week general strike, it had got no support. This resolution was well thought out and was met by approval from the Doncaster branches. They argued in its support, and appealed to the platform, the Council and the Executive not to reject this motion unless they had a strategy equally as good - or any strategy at all would be better than what we had been getting of late. It was pointed out that the leadership can't expect us to keep muddling through with no direction. Doncaster was fed up with having every plan we ever suggest slapped down and at the same time being offered nothing as an alternative.

We had proposed a blockage of London and had been turned down. We had proposed an occupation of the stock exchange and had been turned down. We had proposed surprise sorties into Nottingham and had been turned down. The sharp end of the dispute was the pickets - the continuation of the dispute was only visible to the public through the presence of our pickets, letting renewed picketing perspectives die was as good as letting the strike die. Morale was very low, initiatives must be forthcoming. Turning to the resolution in hand, it was declared obvious to all shades of council opinion that the NUM cannot win the dispute without the support of the rest of the Trade Union Movement. Other sections of the working class must step forward into the breach along side of the NUM.

We couldn't wait for the TUC. We needed key sections, factories, docks, shipyards and general workplaces out with us, that meant we should take the initiative with direct appeals. Perhaps preparing a date for the start of a series of one day strikes and guerilla disruptions right across industry in support of the miners and the right for all trade unionists to organise.

The platform was united in telling us how impractical it all was. We couldn't even get Yorkshire as a county to take one day of action, the most we could get was financial support. North Yorkshire delegates rose to tell us it wasn't only impractical, it was dangerous and could lose us the support that we had. When it came to the vote 19 branches voted for it including every Doncaster branch, with the rest of the council against it.

The next item resulted from the grim situation of the finance in the area. A cut back somewhere had to take place and that was the truth, however the plan that was presented went right to the bone of picketing activity. It was the worst possible way to plan cuts and went as follows: henceforth all allocation of monies would be based on numbers of branch members, and not actual activists in the field. A total sum per week for picket activities was to be fixed which could not be increased choose how many pickets volunteered or actually went on the lines. If there were more pickets than the global sum then pickets would picket for free or go home.

Branches were to be allocated on the basis of their card vote. We were against this method pointing out that a big semi-active branch like Kellingly who could turn out few pickets would get more money, perhaps four or five times as much money, than a small active branch like Goldthorpe who turn out as many, if not more, pickets than Kellingly. The delegate from the small but highly active Training Branch pointed out that on this basis he couldn't afford to put hardly any of his pickets in the field.

The Financial Secretary warned that if something wasn't done we could get to a situation where money ran out entirely, and between now and then we were in for some stormy weather.

Armthorpe proposed and Hatfield seconded that the payments be made on the basis of activists. When put to the vote that resolution got 17 votes including all the Doncaster branches, the rest of the council was against it.

(It should be noted that hardship money was allocated on the basis of members and not activists, obviously a man on strike was on just as much hardship whether he picketed or not, food parcels were allocated on hardship basis also and not simply to activists, had it not been so a very real division would have been created.)

The Hatfield and Armthorpe branches had not been thinking of themselves in putting forward such a resolution since their size left them more or less the same as before. The resolution was motivated on behalf of the small active branches like the Doncaster winders, Carcroft workshops and Goldthorpe and Highgate, and the heroic Training Branch.

At the following Doncaster panel meeting, it was decided to resolve the situation ourselves. After much argument on how to equalise it, the branches agreed to take a per capita reduction based on the card vote. The biggish pits would take a reduction of over £100 per week in order to keep the usual number of pickets going out from the smaller branches.

Council Meeting 8th February and the NEC report given by Johnny Weaver touched on a spectre which would loom to engulf us all, although this was quite unexpected at that time. A Question had been raised about a so called proposal from South Wales for a return to work without any settlement. The idea we were told had originated in a remark of a Welsh staff member and had anyway been taken out of context. The Welsh Area was later bitterly to refute that it had been their official policy and was simply the view of one man which had been seized on by many other areas. The NEC confirmed that this was not a proposal that would ever be contemplated.

The next resolution was from Armthorpe.

Nottingham Area - Armthorpe:

This Armthorpe branch of the NUM demand that our Area Officials start a leafletting campaign against the Nottinghamshire renegades who are destroying the unity of the NUM.

This was something the Doncaster branches had argued for on behalf of our striking Notts comrades for some time. Hatfield seconded it and Askern and Goldthorpe spoke in favour of it. The platform opposed it, with an argument (or waffle, depending on how you view it) which basically said sit tight, do nowt and the scab area might go away of its own accord. When it came to the vote all of the Doncaster branches were in favour, the rest of the council against.

On the 14th February 1985 came news of a legal judgement aimed at hog-tying the whole of our efforts, an emergency Council meeting was told of a new legal action against the South Wales area. A South Wales judge made history and a new piece of law. Prior to his judgement the law had meant something quite different. According to this new judgement six pickets only was to be the law everywhere, demonstrations in any trade dispute are now banned. The primary target then as always was union funds. It was a long stride down the road of making picketing illegal. Any more than six pickets at a road side was henceforth 'ipso facto' to be 'intimidation' and illegal.

The proceedings were commenced on January 2nd and by the following Monday a new law, without any parliamentary discussion or say so, had been created (a suitable answer to any first year Law exam on who makes the law?) The judge, in looking for a cue, couldn't find anything

65

in Parliamentary legislation. Instead he went back to some 18th century court judgement about men standing at the side of the road - 'Even if silent but with glaring looks' would be intimidation of itself.

Given this judgement Yorkshire was more vulnerable since the picketing had had greater co-ordination. If we had as an area contested every writ against us the advice was that the judge would put an injunction on every pit in the area and subsequently we would lose all control of funds, hardship and everything.

Following the South Wales judgement, our lawyers were given dispensation to address the council and give advice, we listened in silence, as we were urged to yield on the points held against Wales in the hope of forestalling yet more far reaching actions against Yorkshire.

We had injunctions pending against 11 pits, so we accepted that at those collieries neither the branch officials or the committee would co-ordinate mass pickets at their pits. Only six pickets would be in attendance at those sites. At all other collieries we would only pay six pickets, if more turned up that was outside the control of the union and the scabs and their legal advisers would have to prove the NUM as such was organising it. Later of course, in places like Edlington the women of the community took to mass picketing, at others old retired members and youngsters and even unemployed. It is a tactic to remember for the future, but at that time was communally spontaneous rather than thought out at Barnsley, who despite criticism were in point of fact trying to sustain our action in the best way they saw it.

Of course we knew it as a delaying tactic, and that the scabs and their Tory legal backers would soon be trying to block us from even limited actions.

The Ordinary Council Meetings

Hatfield had two resolutions.

We call upon the Yorkshire Area Council to insist that all future National Conferences be held in Sheffield

We were fed up with our representatives trying to run away from the coalfields and the miners. We wanted them accessible, we were also against the unnecessary expenditure and aura of a 'trip' present at these functions, rather than a day or week of serious work. The resolution was passed, nay problem. However the second one over which we again expected nay problem was to get a rough ride.

Members dismissed during dispute.

This Hatfield Main branch NUM wish to reaffirm that one of the conditions on which we return to work is the reinstatement of all NUM members who have been sacked for taking part in strike activities.

A number of branches got up to try and talk the resolution down. Briscoe said it was 'too wide.' The union had said some of these people have acted off their own bat and it's their own fault.

Grimethorpe said that he wasn't usually on the side of Hatfield resolutions but on this occasion felt that we had an obligation to these lads who've lost their jobs.

Henry Daly, the North Yorkshire panel president, said on the other hand we aren't strong enough to fight for this. 'A drift back to work will take the members back and leave us and the sacked men outside.' What was necessary he argued was a return to work and then ask for talks.

Johnny Stones for Frickley said he didn't like the way things were sounding. There was back tracking starting already.

Jack Taylor called upon Hatfield to withdraw the resolution, it shouldn't really be on the agenda he said, 'it is Yorkshire area policy already.' But he also said 'Those who've gone out and done things not by union instruction can't be defended.' A straw poll had been conducted by the other Doncaster branches and they quietly urged that I withdraw it, since if we went to the vote we would lose and then Yorkshire wouldn't have an 'amnesty first' policy. Following this council meeting, the men of Doncaster went back to their pits to prepare schemes for supporting the sacked men, or in some cases to resolve not to return until the sacked men were taken on. The writing was very clearly on the wall.

The next Council Meeting saw a whole stream of resolutions from North Yorkshire calling upon us to abandon the strike immediately.

They were in the name of Woolley, Sharlston, South Yorkshire Winders, Wistow (on behalf of Selby as a whole), Ledstone Luck (seconded by Manton), Barrow, Kellingly, and Glasshoughton. Some said the majority were already back at work and if we failed to organise a return the branches as a whole were going back themselves. In the face of all this the platform put forward the following resolution 'while noting the fears of the council which will be conveyed to the next NEC meeting.

This Yorkshire Area of the NUM reaffirm its position and in the light of the situation in the coalfield will continue to strive to reach a negotiated settlement.

We ask our members to continue their magnificent support in order to bring about this end, and that the Area Council will continue to monitor the situation in order to maintain unity.'

When put to the vote it was passed with 3 against, notwithstanding the fact that Barrow, Ledstone Luck, Glasshoughton and Kellingly said they might go back Monday choose what, and the fact that 80% were already back at Shireoaks and Selby.

After the meeting things happened very quickly. The meeting of March heard of the NEC meeting which had lasted several hours and turned itself inside out in the agony of the situation. The Board were not going to budge and had hardened their stance, the areas were wavering. Northumberland announced 60% had gone back to work believing that they could get an amnesty after a return to work. In Durham, floods of men were going back; Easington announced it would go back Monday 'under protest'; Kent was still solid and cried 'stick it out'; North Derbyshire, Cumberland and Leicester, the situation was no longer tenable. The balance fell to South Wales and Yorkshire although the position in Scotland was unclear. (As it turned out the Scottish miners had more belly for continuing the strike then even we in Doncaster had. Following the conference decision to return the Scottish Area doggedly refused to surrender and carried on the strike in an effort to get an amnesty for the victimised men.) In Wales the leadership said if we don't do something 'We're going to make scabs of 19,000 good men.' We were at the 'end of the road'. Yorkshire's position was reaffirmed, but we were looking, following our last council meeting, for an honourable settlement and an amnesty.

The Midlands agreed that the NACODS offer looked better now than it had done before. . . .the trouble is it is no longer on offer. Nottingham argued that we had come too far now and risked too much, an amnesty must come before a settlement.

Bell for COSA said a mass national meeting had given him one week more. The NEC then called a Special Delegate Conference at which Areas must submit resolutions on the current situation.

When it came for Yorkshire to decide its input, the vote was tight, those wishing for a return to work without settlement actually beating on a show of hands the platform resolution to stick out for an amnesty (31 for, 38 against). When it came to a call for a card vote, those calling to stay out just won the day (561 to 557). The Special Delegate Conference, despite this, did not go our way and the national vote was to march back without settlement. But the conference had voted for more than that. It had ruled that the struggle continued. The implication was that plans for guerilla disruption and wildcats would be enacted. We were going back to work to continue the fight, not call it off, and the overtime ban would stay on.

When it was reported back to Yorkshire there was an air of feeling that we should stand out, but the platform said to be practical, we couldn't stand against a conference decision. But in fact 7 branches did vote not to accept the conference's decision. When it was finalised some of us were furious, the air of 'it all being over' permeated everything, despite the resolve to keep the ban on and spread guerilla disruption. Outside the Miners Offices, the pickets swarmed and the press waited to crow how it 'was all over' and the miners were defeated. On emerging from the Hall I made the well publicised (since the end of the strike) statement 'There'll be no coal turned in Yorkshire. The gaffers will wish we were on strike for we'll play merry hell with them!'

It wasn't simply a spontaneous outburst, it was determination to tell the men and the public at large that we hadn't voted to give up the fight, we had voted (reluctantly) to change tactics. It was essential that we didn't seem to be crawling back. Of course it wasn't long before the 'back to work' lobby became the 'back to normal working' lobby and that call would eventually be answered. Branches were pushed out into the wide economic waters, sink or swim, profitability or closure. In that mad whirlpool which followed branches had to struggle to survive, turning coal became a lifeline for many Yorkshire branches determined that our union would not go to the wall. In such a climate, the memory of that bold statement 'There'll be no coal turned in Yorkshire' hung like the biggest wrong prediction of all time, as coal spewed out from South Yorkshire and Doncaster in a deliberate effort to buy time for re-organisation. Some have said it rates with the Captain of the Titanic saying 'I don't think it looks too serious.' Of course it looks out of place, tactics change, the clock does not always say 12, and at this moment it is the wrong statement, for that time it was the right one, although many knew even then that they had no intention of building a guerilla campaign. It was simply the first step in ditching all resistance.

The return, when it came, was raggy. Hatfield and Armthorpe stayed out and continued to picket. Kent was still in the field and calling pits out.

Branches solid to the end tore themselves apart as to whether to defy conference decisions and respect these last ditch pickets, or whether to get the agony over and go to work as instructed by Area. It was a torture for many and one which sowed ultimately disunity, when previously a tight bond had prevailed for 12 months. Whichever, at the time the struggle continued, motivated for the very best of reasons.

The Doncaster Panel 9th March 1985

was a thorough going inquest on the ragged return to work. Goldthorpe said they had spoken at the Area council to stop out but nobody else had done so. It wasn't quite true since Hatfield had seconded the proposition, but Taylor wouldn't allow any debate on it, saying the vote would be either for or against the recommendation to go back. At the end of the meeting the Doncaster delegates debated whether or not it would be possible for us to go it alone with Kent, and the consensus was no. (We were unaware of Scotland's continued resistance at this time).

Armthorpe said they felt they had been betrayed, their pickets abused and insulted and in some cases assaulted. Every branch in Doncaster had stated it was their branch policy not to return without an amnesty for the sacked men, and that was the policy of the Doncaster panel.

Meantime, at the Area Council meeting of 18th March the struggle for disruption at work was still to be talked about. This came to the fore during discussions on Area Consultative Committees. We were supposed to be carrying out a policy of 'gaan canny' and the NEC had given permission for participation in these Committees.

Silverwood

That this Yorkshire Area of the NUM ballots its members on the following:

The Area Incentive Scheme be suspended until all its members who have been dismissed for actions during the 84/85 dispute have been reinstated or until such time as determined by Area Council.

Further to this the Yorkshire Area Officials request the NEC to recommend the support of other areas of the NUM for similar action to be taken.

Silverwood since the end of the strike had relentlessly pursued a policy of seeking action on the sacked men, and emerged as a vanguard branch of the entire area on a whole range of trade union and political subjects, at that time.

It was a strong resolution which showed the will to continue the fight, but it was dangerous. If the ballot had been lost, it could be taken as waving bye bye to the sacked men. Also it was pointed out by the Doncaster delegates it ought to be unnecessary, we were on a work to rule/gaan canny as it was, and the production of coal ought not to be producing bonuses. The only coal coming out of Yorkshire pits ought to be in the men's boots and no more! Despite this 20 branches voted for it, showing the spirit of resistance was still very alive and strong in our neck of the woods. However we were to be met by a serious contrast.

A series of resolutions calling for an end of the overtime ban and a return to normal working was put down in the name of External Services, Barnsley Road Transport, Gasgoine Wood and Ledstone Luck. Others joined in;

Nostell - We didn't go back to work victorious, we went back defeated and we ought to accept that situation.

The Goldthorpe, Hatfield, Askern, and Bentley branches spoke against the retreat, arguing about jobs, about young 'uns on the dole, about the overtime and coal production shutting pits elsewhere. Kilnhurst argued that those who were looking for seven shifts a week should look at their poor mates who weren't getting any shifts a week for they had been sacked in a struggle to defend jobs. If we couldn't stop on our five shifts and get paid in the cause it was disgusting.

When put to the vote 14 branches voted for a return to normal working (all the North Yorkshire branches).

Delegates Report 19th March 1985

Platform again suggested that the same two as last year go on this occasion.

Financial Report

KH gave us a brief financial report, dealing with some of the income we had received during the strike (!) and the limited ability to send out allocations to branches and meet the demands on the union.

The National Union, because of the courts, has no money whatever. The Yorkshire Area is having to pay itself on a great number of items it ought to get from National. It will not be able to go on for ever, and the Yorkshire Area could soon find itself in a situation which was very grim indeed.

Questions

I asked if I had heard correctly that we had been sent, and accepted dues from the Scabs, who were working while we were on strike, if so it was an absolute farce. Briscoe said we were obliged to do so!

Nottingham Area - Expulsion Demand

Two resolutions came on the agenda for the expulsion of Notts. One from Dearne Valley, the other from Clayton West. The arguments from many sides of the room were to do just that. Notts did not want to be in our union, were using us and giving nothing. They were a fifth column. We couldn't sit back and leave them alone because they were going to come after us, they wanted to rule the union after extracting its teeth or else to break the union. We couldn't wait any longer, the expulsion was vital and Now!

The platform informed us it was already Yorkshire area policy but we couldn't expel them, only the National Union could do that and they were sitting on it. I pointed out that the last time I came with a resolution I was told it was already Yorkshire area policy and there was no need to move it. That resolution had been No Return Without Amnesty so if it was all the same could we just have the resolution moved and let's move on it just to be sure.

When we did so the vote was unanimous.

Transfer of Branch to Notts Area - Shireoaks

This resolution expressed determination to resist any moves regarding transfers from the Yorkshire Area to Notts, both NCB and NUM areas. Basically it came about because of strong rumours that the Board intended to ship Shireoaks and Manton out of the Yorkshire NCB area into the Notts NCB area. About 95% of both sets of men live in Notts and many of them had worked since early on in the strike. The branch itself was determined to resist the trend. When put to the vote the council again unanimously agreed to support them in that fight.

Closure of the Rothwell and Highgate Branches

The above was noted and a vote of thanks given to the long and faithful service given by the members and officials of those branches.

South Yorkshire Defence Campaign - Demonstration - Kinsley Drift

I personally had expected no problems whatever with this resolution and had along with the Kinsley delegate given out leaflets about the demonstration the day before and at that meeting.

Of course about half way through the strike Briscoe and the Executive Committee in Yorkshire had decided to have nothing to do with that Committee. We had thought that it had all been a misunderstanding and the work of the committee had proven its worth.

Kinsley's Resolution read as follows

This branch of the NUM calls upon the Area Council to support and mobilise for the National Demonstration called by the South Yorks Defence Campaign. The demonstration is calling for amnesty for sacked miners and is Saturday March 30th, assembly 11am at Caborns Corner, Sheffield.

Kinsley's delegate, also anticipating no problems, moved the resolution briefly, saying it was self explanatory and called on everyone to support it. I formally seconded it.

Taylor said if branches wanted to support it it was up to them, but the EC had been against it.

Briscoe then got up and did a blustering Colonel Blimp act, 'Someone had been and put one of these posters up (advertising the demonstration) they have no right, people could be putting anything up here against the union.

'Who's behind this thing? Look at the names on this poster, they're nearly all women! These people are talking about miners but they're not just involved with miners, they've had campaigns about black people. This is the trots, at least three people on this list of speakers are trots!'

(NB: Listed speakers - Jack Collins, Secretary, Kent Area, NUM; Betty Heathfield, Women Against Pit Closures; Richard Caborn, MP; Johnny Moyle, President, Bettshanger, Kent (sacked); Liz French, gaoled miner's wife; Nicky Boyle, Yorkshire miner's wife.)

I must admit to flying right up the wall at such reactionary rubbish. Briscoe had said this campaign could make the union 'feel uncomfortable.' I told him it's not as uncomfortable as laying in a prison cell for fighting for your job and this union. Yes, I had put the poster up, I thought as a member of the union I could put a poster up in our own offices, especially about a campaign to support our jailed comrades. Incidentally I had stuck it besides a number of posters already up, one dealing with meditation, another for Oxfam, these were OK but demonstrations in support of men who fought for this union were not! It was a cause which everyone could identify with. His opinions on 'Trots, or Anarchists or Henry Daly or Howard Wadsworth or some of the strange political animals who inhabit the back of the council chamber (ie Roy Mason, MP) was neither here nor there. We weren't operating a political witch hunt and there were no proscriptions in this union so long as a delegate faithfully carried out the mandate of his branch, Briscoe's prejudices had nothing to do with the issue.

Taylor then informed us that he had in fact been invited to speak but couldn't make it. We aren't against this demonstration, he told us, so long as we don't have to pay anything for it. He then asked the Kinsley delegate to withdraw the resolution in favour of a call from the branches to support this demonstration, without any financial obligation on the area. This Kinsley accepted and when put to the vote the whole council with the single exception of Henry Daly, an official of the North Yorks Panel, and Nostell branch, voted in favour of it. I must admit to feeling a bit sick at some of the things the General Secretary of the area had said.

They were in stark contrast to the comments of the National Secretary, Peter Heathfield. In a letter from the National Union (11th March ref. NO2/PEH/EA) to the South Yorkshire Defence Campaign, he had said:

We welcome, and indeed are most grateful, for the efforts of the South Yorkshire Defence Campaign in helping us achieve our objective and sharing the responsibility of getting the men their jobs back. In so doing we are not only safeguarding the welfare of the men, but also that of their families and communities.

I wish your demonstration every success.
Peter Heathfield.

Area Meetings. . . .Edlington. This again was another source of argument. Edlington simply wanted permission for the panels to hold meetings each week instead of once per month, while we were facing such attacks from the Board in order to keep ourselves informed. It was not to be and the platform wouldn't have it.

When it came to the vote, 28 branches were for and 39 against.

Result of NEC Voting

We had supported J. Stones of Frickley but he was not elected, the 'left' had chosen to support Mr. Dakin of the North Yorkshire coalfield and he was elected along with Briscoe and Taylor.

The Doncaster Panel Meeting of 27th March 85 saw Armthorpe in trouble with the Area officials over their delegate (Gordon Morris) getting the staff to look up various parts of legislation etc., in an effort of finding ways to reinstate their men or prepare evidence for tribunals. The lodge officials were subsequently summoned to Barnsley.

Rossington reported that it had 26 men sacked, 4 of whom had never been charged but were sacked on the basis of a statement from the CID to the NCB.

Bentley reported that they had been on strike for 24 hours, the result of men refusing to carry 6 bolts in and being sent home, everyone else had come out in support. They further reported that a 'mole' in the Thorne Road offices reported that a meeting of top NCB directors had discussed the conduct of branch officials in Doncaster and set up a monitoring brief to watch out for their activities currently. The names of the Bentley Delegate, the Hatfield Delegate and the Goldthorpe Secretary had been mentioned. The main item was whether or not they could get away with sacking them for misconduct.

Edlington had been on strike over plans to get them into the pit earlier than their normal time.

It was agreed that some sort of show would have to be put up as the Board were taking everything off us and still coming back for more. This led to a discussion of the widespread attacks upon the Doncaster coalfield, that the Doncaster coalfield was the only Yorkshire Area which had not had men reinstated. The question was what were we going to do about any of this. It was agreed that all Doncaster branches would agenda for 13th April the question of our response to management attacks in Doncaster.

The Sacked Men's Fund - Ballot

Shortly after this came the result of the ballot on the 50p levy to support our sacked men. It was felt far and wide that coming straight after a year of utter deprivation the idea of a levy was a lot to swallow. It was pointed out that a campaign ought to have been held to make people understand just what was involved here and how vital the levy was. In the event the ballot was 'sprung' presumably in the hope of striking while the iron of resistance was hot. Actually it was badly timed and without a campaign it fell. That aside the results of the ballot in North Yorkshire as opposed to Doncaster are illustrative of the different characters of the leaderships or traditions in the respective areas.

North Yorkshire branches against

Branch	Yes	No	Blank	Spoilt	Total
Glasshoughton	194	211	1	0	406
Sharlston	281	543	0	0	824
Allerton Workshops	111	375	0	0	486
Nostell	173	194	0	0	367
Pontefract	453	536	0	1	990
Allerton Silkstone	414	587	0	8	1,009
North Yorkshire Winders	10	34	1	0	45
Ledstone Luck	148	206	0	3	357
Kellingly	669	791	1	3	1,464
Gasgoine Wood	128	157	0	0	285
Wistow	181	302	0	0	483
Stillingfleet	131	168	0	0	299
Ricall	107	127	0	0	234
North Selby	21	71	0	1	93
Whitmoor	12	53	0	0	65

North Yorkshire branches in favour

Branch	Yes	No	Blank	Spoilt	Total
Fryston	546	96	0	5	642
Acton Hall	286	260	0	5	551
Clayton West	169	77	0	0	246
Emley	80	61	0	0	141
Savile Pit	125	103	5	0	233
Roystone Drift	248	117	0	0	365

Doncaster branches in favour

Branch	Yes	No	Blank	Spoilt	Total
Carcroft Workshops	112	100	1	0	213
Hickleton Main	159	28	0	0	187
Frickley	903	167	7	0	1,077
Brodsworth	917	438	0	3	1,358
Bentley	390	255	1	0	646
Goldthorpe	390	43	0	0	433
Edlington	553	350	0	0	903
Askern	539	289	2	1	831
Rossington	619	438	0	1	1.058
Hatfield Main	533	260	0	0	793
Armthorpe	780	197	1	2	980
Thorne	11	10	0	0	21

Doncaster branches against

Branch	Yes	No	Blank	Spoilt	Total
Doncaster Area Winders	8	35	0	0	43

A narrow majority in Yorkshire voted Yes to the ballot but nationally only 46% did, a fact which the Board never let us forget.

At the council meeting 1st April, we heard that the NEC meeting had received a Midland resolution saying that the overtime ban must come off and a special delegate conference be convened to discuss it.

Within that meeting the Kent Area argued it was all we had left and ought to be kept on. North Derbyshire argued that the ban hadn't saved jobs or pits and was currently stopping our men getting at least five days in. Both SCEBT and Lancs argued that the ban on its own wasn't effective and a number of areas and pits were already working overtime, it was our most loyal people who were suffering. Nottingham had been working overtime, those of our strikers who went back were now being victimised for refusing to work overtime. Yorkshire was against lifting the ban following recent council instructions to that effect. When put to the vote 18 were in favour of taking it off, 5 against, that seems to have been Kent, Durham and Yorkshire (who have 5 votes between them).

Following the report, the platform had no option but to move we now take the ban off. Taylor argued that all principles said it ought to be maintained but it was causing tremendous difficulty. The sacked lads were not getting dole, the redundant men weren't getting dole, and Eaton point blank refused to discuss amnesty while it stayed on. The platform's proposal was seconded by the North Yorkshire Panel president. First to speak against it was South Kirkby, followed by Hatfield and Johnny Stones from Frickley. When it came to the vote the platform's resolution was carried 38 votes to 31 with two Doncaster branches, Goldthorpe and the winders voting to back the platform. There was then a call for a card vote, which went the other way, 454 for calling it off and 652 for keeping it on. Thus we saw not for the first time the independence of the Yorkshire branches, voting against both an NEC and an Area Officials recommendation. Thus armed we would take this mandate to the Special Delegate Conference.

The conference was held on the 2nd April with the NEC recommendation before us. All areas spoke, and finally Sammy Thompson, who made a first class speech outlining the road before us, the pitfalls and dangers, and asking at every juncture just what were we going to do? If there was to be no ban, what was to take its place? There was no answer of course and when we moved to the vote it went 122 for lifting it, 74 against. (Durham, Kent and Yorkshire).

After this the chips came down rapidly. Doncaster was unable to formulate a defence strategy on its own although there were sterling attempts, but the logic became crystal clear. Uneconomic pits would close, we had fired our bolt on that, all the marches and lobbies, petitions and inquiries, even the favourable recommendations of the already weighted review body, would not prevent it.

Doncaster was one of the most unprofitable strife torn coalfields in

Britain. It had been to the last day the strongest, most solid coalfield in Britain, better even that South Wales in percentages for scabs. It stuck out like a sore thumb.

The choice was a difficult one. Carry on the fight in totally unfavourable terrain and die the rapid death, such was the fate of Edlington, a crack regiment in the army of Yorkshire's militants. It couldn't stand the new strategy which was one of trying to get the pits profitable enough to get out of the immediate firing line. It could not as others had done, accept the new bonus deal, bite the bullet and live to fight another day. It closed. Certain heroic native American tribes went the same way following just such a defeat and choice of options. Greed and redundancy fever was a factor, but the overall feature was Edlington's stubborn resistance and determination to fight to the last, which it did. Edlo is gone now, the shaft is filled in and the pulley gear getting dismantled, the empty space is a monument to the wrong tactic, some short sightedness, but bare stubborn class resistance when all seemed lost as well. Edlo men currently employed throughout the new South Yorkshire Area still add mettle to every struggle we engage in, they still stand proud in our ranks.

Others turned round and started to bury the area in coal, not because of the NCB, but to spite them, they would dearly have loved the excuse of closing the coalfield altogether. Doncaster and her militant branches had a cause and a mission, they had to survive. Many started to break records, but before the Board could crow about 'new found co-operation' the self-same pit would down tools and walk out. Production Plus Disruption as I termed it, was evident in the strike statistics, at the same time as the Doncaster pits were breaking all targets, they accounted for fully one half of all disputes in the entire British coalfields put together. On occasion they accounted for two thirds of all days lost. Days of strike action have followed one pit on another, bans and go slows mark the current offensive, despite 'the Doncaster option' bonus scheme.

After the Strike

The independence of action typified by the Doncaster branches before and during the strike continued after, though on this occasion not necessarily by choice, all areas and regions were thrown into their own back yards. The perspective of getting stuck in to turn coal was meant to buy us a breathing space and time for organisational regroupment, but this didn't materialise. Many perceived a paralysis in the National Executive Committee, there was no direction; we waited for a special conference to review the failure of the strike, take stock of what we had left, what ground could be held, what conceded, it never came. Area organisation proved too uneven, too varied to cobble any overall strategy together. The National officials continued to make speeches as if the strike were still on and our army was still in the field. That we were still at war wasn't in question, but we were fighting a different battle on a different field than the one Arthur and Peter seemed to be on.

Into all of this came the most pernicious tendency of all, the 'shut the pit merchants' crazed with redundancy fever, they lived, breathed, loved and would kill for 'Their Redundancy'. Their waking hours were filled with fantasies of pit closures and bags of money. Privately they spoke the language of greed and self interest; publicly they adopted the language of the militant, the strong union man. Production? You were a scab to even mention production, 'no coal turned in Yorkshire. . . .remember?' Flexibility? Delay analysis? 'Stick to union policies!!!' It was among these elements a sacriligious gesture, for they wanted in actual fact no production, more delays, less flexibility, for they wanted neither pit nor union. A bit like the impatient vulture sitting on the cliff, 'sod this waiting for something to die. . . .I'm going to kill something!'

So it was that the class conscious trade union activist had to try and steer a course between defeatism and industrial suicide on one hand and the danger of collaboration on the other. It was not a dichotomy we could ignore, nor petulantly refuse to have any part in. Our day to day contact with the mine and the miners, and often violent ideological struggle over which way forward if any, had to be joined in as realistic, pragmatic and yet principled way as possible, if the union branch was to keep any

81

relevance to the problems being faced by our members.

Branches fought hard in their own back yards, negotiated what deals they could, struggled to prove our relevancy to the members who rewarded the union by continued membership and loyalty. The initiative had not been passed to the branches; it fell to the branches since none seemed to be emanating from elsewhere.

Much later, when the dust settled somewhat, when the smoke of battle cleared, those NUM branches were still standing, although many had been forced to concede ground on new contracts etc. We felt we had done well, bending at times in order not to break. This wasn't the view of the National Officials, however, and branches were heavily criticised for 'breaking ranks'. For our part we felt the National Office remote and out of touch with the monumental battle we had been through to keep our organisation together. The Doncaster branches in particular were rattled by those from the less combative areas of Yorkshire who chanced upon the 'Doncaster Option'. (This was a new incentive contract which radically altered the terms of the area incentive scheme, primarily it shifted the terms of the agreement away from the Area Office and guidelines. It was, claimed the Coal Board, designed for the specific conditions of the hitherto low productivity Doncaster coalfield. It placed great emphasis on coal production and penalised running delays.) They used the 'Doncaster Option' as a means of tarnishing the fiery reputation of the Doncaster men while distracting attention from their own ineffectiveness.

The Doncaster Option became a folk myth and an endless source of academic theorising; mostly wildly misconceived and factually inaccurate. In any case turning our efforts to increasing production was by no means our independent idea, we had to be pulled kicking and screaming to even accept the idea that coal production had anything to do with us. The Doncaster pits had never made a habit of high productivity even when there was no dispute, no conscious effort to restrict it. What had maddened the Board was the fact the Doncaster pits frequently turned less coal when they were working than others turned when on strike or overtime bans.

However, having been isolated by the national conference decision, first to return to work and then to call off even minimal resistance and having been similarly isolated by the same decisions of council and refusal to countenance other forms of action, we were then all summoned before the Area (British Coal) Director, who laid his cards on the table. MacGregor had told him Doncaster had the highest level of disputes anywhere in Britain. Frequently all top ten positions were occupied by Doncaster and rarely ever less than the top five:-

National Statistics for Tonnages Lost Through Disputes During the Quarter Ended 29th March 86.
South Yorkshire was top of the National League with 38 disputes. The rate of tonnes lost per 1,000 tonnes of saleable output was 20.35. The Area was responsible for 41% of the total number of disputes. 5 South Yorkshire pits had the heaviest tonnage lost and 6 the highest number of disputes. Doncaster had the highest rate of absenteeism, double the national average. Even the Deputies were twice as high as the national average. Doncaster had the lowest productivity and the greatest loss makers in Britain. Mac could see 'no reason' for the existence of the Doncaster coalfield as it stood. When challenged on Doncaster's huge reserves he commented that the Firth of Clyde contains gold but nobody could commercially extract it.

So the chips were down. Agree to new devices to increase production or face closure. The Area Production Manager Mr White said with an ashen face 'and if you think we're bluffing, test us and see'. They weren't bluffing and Edlington, a crack regiment of the Doncaster army was killed stone dead, stubbornly refusing to accept new bonus arrangements. They were in consequence paid no bonus whatever, so turned no coal, so were executed.

A great many of us were perilously close to the edge also, the new bonus scheme would stimulate coal production and give workers a vested interest in minimising delays. We were warned accept this contract or stand the consequences. We needed, for all the causes we believed in and our own place in fighting for them, to live to fight another day. Frickley was the only pit big enough, productive enough, to withstand the trend and carry on the area scheme.

The tactic of 'production plus disrupton' and industrial armalite plus the ballot box, ensured the statistics would show that while the Doncaster pits were edging towards records they collectively accounted for half of all other coalfield stoppages put together. Of the 12 collieries with heaviest tonnage lost (52 weeks ended 29th March) 2 of them were from

Doncaster, of those with the highest number of disputes 7 of them were from Doncaster.

A strange period of non-war, non-peace, shot through with contradictory elements developed during 86 and 87. While pit closures could still be fought, and even on occasion won, individual offers of redundancy were unstoppable. Pits were closed and men transferred to others, allowing men at the older end of the receiving pits' workforce to go redundant. The workforce's age dropped below an average of 32 - pit rag ups and local demands seemed increasingly futile under the new hard line management. Local lodges struggled to raise productivity to keep on their feet and in the ring. Production, often under the conscious initiation of local militants and branch officials, rose phenomenally - losses were cut back to well below the expected figures, while individual areas broke European coal records, and individual collieries broke world records, often by easy margins.

Despite the air of hard nosed management, many Area directors were well pleased and believed their brief of efficiency and production was being fulfilled. Orders had gone down the line to managers to back off some of the more contentious issues, while at Area Disputes Committee (the third level of the conciliation process) a number of disputes were still being settled in favour of the union.

The systematic stopping of collieries and the Area in protest at the continued victimisation of men sacked during the 84/85 conflict took some of the gloss off the performance figures and irritated the Area director, but in many ways he could pass the buck for these down to Hobart House where the fate of the sacked men rested.

As men regained a bit of bargaining clout and their individual financial positions started to consolidate, so the number of rag ups increased and started to assume pre-strike proportions. Despite the constant complaints from local Board chiefs and attempts by lodge officials to channel the disputes into more constitutional action, at certain collieries they were endemic. Thus the overall position was stable with losses dropping dramatically, both Board and union announced a bright future.

At national level the position was very much different. A state of open hostility had continued between Board chiefs and the national officials. Even the push for 'new realism' coming from the Communist Party influenced areas and the inclusion of the whole NEC in negotiations didn't improve the relationship. The union had not negotiated a pay rise since 82 and every increase since that time had been unilaterally imposed (although lately with the endorsement of the minute UDM).

Relations hit the skids dramatically when plans emerged to lop another 50,000 jobs from the industry (75,000 had gone since the end of the strike) via the introduction of 6 day coal production, continental shift work and in the Geordie coalfields 9 .5 hour shift work. The planned, great increase in machine running time, to easy breaking of existing production figures with a much smaller workforce.

Board chiefs in London had hoped to circumvent the National Office and allow Area deals to be struck, thin end of the wedge fashion, thus hoping Arthur would wake up one morning and find many of the coalfields already working a 6 day cycle. The Margam protest was the one that hit the headlines and for a time an internecine struggle developed between South Wales and the National Office, the latter pointing out that the matter was a national issue and not a parochial one, the former in the spirit of new pragmatism feeling it was fighting for the very existence of the Welsh coalfield.

The Board for its part avoided contact and discussion with the NEC like the plague and determined to push decisions and authority to Areas and thus circumvent Arthur and the union as a national entity. The National Conference of 87 countered that with a recommendation of opposition to any extension of the working day or week, and a decision to put the matter to a national ballot.

The question, however, which went straight to the heart and was to lead to a massive explosion of anger, first in the old Doncaster Area, then spreading like lightning into South Yorkshire and North Yorkshire, was the Board's new disciplinary code.

Though the Board were later to claim the code had been on the drawing board with the full knowledge of the union since 81, to the rank and file, and even colliery management, it was an unwanted and deliberately provocative imposition.

The existing practice made a strict separation between disciplinary offences, ie breaches of the M & Q and industrial relations problems which were the subject of colliery dispute procedures and conciliation agreements (though the latter were still 'informal').

Rumours started to circulate that the Board had developed a new code of practice which clearly aimed at outlawing all trade union practice as we had known it. Stories abounded from Notts and Derbyshire collieries of Lodge secretaries suspended or even sacked for pinning up NUM notices or for getting involved in arguments away from the pit on holidays or at weekends. At the same time there was a flurry of correspondence between Peter Heathfield (General Secretary NUM) and Kevin Hunt, the Head of Industrial Relations at Hobart House. The word was that the new code was being issued to managers, yet another imposition carried through without prior consultation or agreement by the union.

The correspondence from Hunt seemed to concede that they could not impose the code unilaterally, and therefore the impression was drawn that it was not to be implemented. The National Officials apparently consigned it to low on the list of priorities although the National Conference had given them instuctions to oppose it; they reasoned that 6 day working would be the flash point, and the other issue was not an immediate concern. It was, however, soon to be so.

At Hatfield, for example, two incidents put the matter directly on the agenda. One involved a team of heading men working in thick mud attempting to repair a broke machine. To do this a man and a fitter had to work beneath a sacked up section of the machine in a two foot working height, which of course necessitated laying flat in a swamplike mix of mud and oil leaking from the machine. The men demanded to do the job, then ride the pit to wash the oil from their skin, and change their overalls for the following shift. If the charge overman was a meanie, he would normally fix them up with a time wasting job on the pit top till lowse - or if in a good mood let them go home. This customary practice was obstructed by the intervention of a recently arrived undermanager who would allow only the fitter plus one of the workmen to ride. The men contended that they had all taken turns under the machine, shovelling out, and therefore all should ride. Negotiations between the undermanager and a branch official reached deadlock and the men rode the pit in dispute. A small, not unusual incident. The branch official then rode into the pit to inspect the job site, and arranged a meeting with the undermanager for the Friday to take up the case through the normal dispute procedure. The following day (Thursday) a similar dispute arose and an hour before lowse the men ragged up and came out of the pit to present themselves, in their soaked and wretched condition, to the undermanager. But by this time more sinister developments were afoot, all of the men had been sent a registered letter, telling them that this constituted a written warning, they were in breach of their contract of employment, had left work without permission (a breach of the new code), the offence was to be entered on their records and any other occurrence could lead to their dismissal.

In the second case, a fitter had questioned his deployment from a priority job to one previously deemed less important. An argument ensued and the local disputes procedure entered into, after the intervention of a branch committee man, the fitter reluctantly accepted the deployment and successfully completed the job. The following day he received a registered letter, he had to see the colliery engineer for failing to carry out his deployment (a breach of the new code).

The fat was perilously close to the fire, the branch officials arranged a hurried meeting with the manager, while preparing for a mass meeting which would agenda possible strike action against the introduction of the new code at Harfield. The pit seemed ready to be first in action over the code. The brink was not crossed though, as the manager agreed to suspend the letters and warnings 'pending an investigation'. The letters from Hunt, and conflicting instructions from Area had caused the local gaffer to be unsure footed, he would await developments elsewhere.

Meantime news was circulating, though unclearly, that a secretary had been suspended in North Yorkshire for breach of the code. (It turned out to be Ted Scott, secretary of Selby's Stillingfleet branch.)

At Frickley the gaffer decided to press ahead and three sets of letters went out, one for an argument over men taking their bait 'late' (they worked to complete a job through the customary bait stand) and were sent out of the pit. In another a group of men were said to have left the job early prior to the annual holiday (the 'job and knock' custom prior to a holiday, though not an agreement, is what the American business schools refer to as an 'indulgency pattern' and was very common in the Doncaster Area). The registered letters went out demanding interviews on an individual (ie disciplinary rather than industrial relations) basis. The Frickley men, recognising this as part of the new code and not the usual procedure, refusing to seem party to the code by attending its procedures, refused to go. This was followed by the immediate suspension of the men required for interview. (Another feature of the new code).

Frickley's meeting was a massive rejection of compliance with the new 'ethic' of jackboot management. The branch, though typical of the Doncaster tradition, and usually top voter in all strike ballots in the Area, had been historically constitutional. The mood of the Frickley men was on this occasion hard even by Doncaster standards. A plea from the officials to strike and approach the South Yorkshire panel for support was massively rejected in favour of immediate picketing out of their Doncaster comrades.

From the nightshift on Wednesday 15th July, Frickley pickets turned out at every Doncaster colliery and the pits stood to a man, branch officials supervising the policy 'Don't cross picket lines'. Hatfield and Rossington, both having EC members, called an emergency panel meeting while at their own emergency branch meetings resolved to respect Frickley' lines. The aim of the emergency panel meeting was to win support from all South Yorkshire for the action, though there were those in the Frickley ranks who suspected a 'get out' was being sought. Throughout the action there were elements of 'worker autonomism' in the Frickley ranks and a feeling that the rank and file could handle the struggle without even the informal and previously militant union structure such as the panel. The meeting was heavily lobbied, and some expressed a view that it was to the members directly that they shoould be going as they had had enough of 'officials of any sort, always keeping the lid on'. Despite this, the reception for Frickley's case was warm and comradely. Branches in turn expressing the minimal application of the code at their respective pits and the resolve that this was a battle which must be fought. That opinion forbye many expressed the view that all-out unlimited action was beyond the mettle of their men. More limited actions were debated, but the question was fudged in favour of support now, spreading the dispute to the North Yorkshire pits via an appeal to their forthcoming panel meeting, and take the question of length of action as it came.

The resolution to the South Yorkshire panel which I had hurriedly drawn up
through the course of the debate attempted to include the majority

views being expressed. When put it was unanimously accepted.

It is the opinion of the South Yorkshire Panel that the coalfield will continue to be subject to disruption until such time as the Coal Board withdraws its unilaterally imposed disciplinary code.

This Panel supports the stand made by the Frickley branch and calls upon all its member branches to convene emergency meetings to discuss the situation.

We further request an informal meeting with the North Yorkshire Panel to review the situation.

However, the Board were not the only people threatened by the potential of rank and file action. Certain elements on the NEC were scared shitless of the prospect of Area strikes undermining the limited National Action which had been voted upon in a nationwide ballot, but hadn't as yet been acted upon.

Arthur had been in touch with the Area Officials to say the problem was a national one and should be responded to in that way. The officials were reminded that they were part of the NEC and the NEC had been given a strict instruction by the annual conference as to which way to respond to the disciplinary code.

The EC for its part expressed the fear that the Board could well make a couple of amendments to the National Code and conclude an agreement, leaving Ted Scott high and dry. However, we were assured that Scott and Paul Whetton (an official of the Nottingham coalfield, like Scott victimised for union activity) would be raised with ACAS and would be features of negotiation with the Board.

The EC subsequently demanded that the National Executive act upon the ballot result if no satisfaction was reached by the 14th September (under the new law, the last date when the ballot result could be implemented).

Meantime the joint panels met and debated the response from the branches. The response indicated the extent to which the issue had now cooled off, and a number of branches still bemoaned the lack of action from Stillingfleet. However, as the results came in an interesting shift

89

in strength of reaction was shown. Of the nine Doncaster pits, two wanted all out indefinite strike action; one wanted day strikes; two said they would match whatever Stillingfleet were prepared to do so long as they did it for a week first. Two wanted overtime bans without flexibility or safety cover; two wanted overtime bans with flexibility.

Of eight South Yorkshire pits five wanted weeks of strike action; one wanted overtime ban graduating to week strikes; one wanted overtime ban without flexibility; one wanted overtime ban with safety cover.

All resolved that if the national union did not act, the branches in Yorkshire would.

As it turned out the NEC 'pissed the ballot result against the wall' by calling the most ineffectual 'action' imaginable, which in turn steadily wore down the determination of the membership to fight. It was a betrayal.

A Mine of Misinformation

Leftist comments on the strike and the pickets, as we said in opening, have in nearly all cases been wrong politically and incorrect in point of facts.

The inaccuracies of the Marxist groups, particularly the self-designated Trotskyist groups, are legion. Situationists were far from immune from the self-righteous prescriptions invariably based on half truths or no truths at all. *Miner Conflicts, Major Contradictions* (by BM Combustion): *The first flying pickets which were not controlled by the NUM, the saboteurs of working pits; the organisers of the motorway "chaos"....* As if the calling together of the pickets, the organised sortie onto the motorway, the spontaneous attacks upon scab buildings were to be counterposed to 'the NUM' which is somehow not the members involved in all these actions but something outside, personal and yet inanimate. *To be sure the first flying pickets initially opposed by the Stalinist Jack Taylor were set up by mass meetings of the miners.* It would make you scream! All pickets were derived from mass meetings of the miners. Jack Taylor is not a 'Stalinist' by anyone's definition. The decision on the first day's picketing is as explained in this book a question of strategic and historic initiative and not some attempt to prevent all picketing for ever and a day. The question was never whether to picket but where, some of the Doncaster pickets, under the leadership of Armthorpe's 'hole in the wall gang', got impatient with the success of the strike in Yorkshire and subsequent no need to picket that county and went over the border to find some action in Nottingham. It was not some popular push for picketing as against Jack Taylor et al's refusal to organise it. Such is a plain misrepresentation of history, or perhaps the invention of a new history more suited to the expectations of the Situationists and SWPers who invented the myth.

We were the first branch in Doncaster Area to go out picketing into Nottingham and we went to Harworth colliery. And that was the only time I've seen a trade union official on a picket line. The Doncaster Area agent came on that picket line and asked us to withdraw back to Doncaster because a deal had been struck with Chadburn relating to the ballot, and

91

we should only send a token lobby of four men to every branch.
(Socialist Worker)

The numbers of branch officials, particularly in Doncaster, who picketed, led marches and charges, were beaten and arrested and some jailed, the Area officials and national officials at Orgreave and elsewhere who were beaten and arrested, shows the slanderous lie of the above paragraph. The whole myth grows and keeps on growing from a simple breach of discipline, no matter how understandable on the first day, while everybody else is held back by 'the Stalinists' (actually the Yorkshire Area of the NUM had not one CP Delegate to the council or member of the Executive Committee in the whole strike, but what's politics got to do with creation of a myth?)

While the soft left have sought to berate the miners for 'picking a fight' with the government, at the wrong time, over the wrong issue etc., Ian Macgregor lays the whole thing open by outlining how he and Thatcher planned the whole thing. The entire book (*The Enemy Within*) is mapped out in terms of a battle plan in preparation awaiting for the right moment. He talks of the 81 backdown as being 'the wrong time' for the Board. There was very little coal in stock. . . .The TGWU's grip was still too tight.

In terms of our pickets in Nottingham, he admits that they were very effective and consequently dreamed up the 'back to work movement' as a means of opening up a fifth column in the solid areas no matter how tiny. This would cause the pickets to fall back into the home areas in an attempt to render them sound again. In talking of his strategy to open up this second front he concedes the overall loyalty of the vast bulk of our members, but outlines the need to cause a crack. Of course the press determined to exaggerate the crack into a chasm and later talked of a split and the union 'crumbling' (at its worst about 7% of Yorkshire miners were back at work by the last week of the strike.)

Macgregor is completely paranoid and cannot match the overwhelming support for the strike with his fanatical belief in Capitalism and the notion that it is a system that everybody wants. The explanation was intimidation.

But at the core of most of the trouble was a hardened group of miners who had obviously been trained well in advance in techniques designed to force dissenters into line. We had reports of these cadres mainly of young miners based in Doncaster area being created and trained ù but we did not realise how effective they could be until the battle for Nottingham was on in earnest.

As the strike went on so Mac's nightmares became more obsessive.

A sinister mob of almost uniformed anarchists led by a woman appeared at one stage and caused a great deal of damage in Yorkshire.

Despite the fact that the police and the Home Office denied any truth in the story it remained in Macgregor's brain, which is probably where it came from.

Everyone it seems was in on the conspiracy. By 15th March only 11 pits were working, the reason for this being that the police were too soft, too unwilling or incapable of stopping our pickets getting through.

That is why I sought to see the Prime Minister and the Home Secretary "boiling with righteous indignation",' he invoked '. . .the stereotyped image of the typical American cop' 'who was needed on the scene.' I put it as vehemently as I could. "I never thought I would be sitting here in the UK wishing I had a bunch of good untidy American cops out there." In brief it was rough stuff against the pickets he wanted. 'I suggested that were this America the authorities would have called out the National Guard by now.'

It was after this advocation that the National Reporting Centre was brought to life.

The conspiracy didn't stop with the police but went right through the NCB who hated him, he says, and the Civil Service who had tried to block him getting the job in the first place.

It did not take me long to discover that the Civil Service at the Dept. . . .perhaps more so than any other nationalised industry enjoyed a happy relationship, and that they have a long history of collectively repelling boarders. It was only on the insistence of the Prime Minister that he got the job at all.

BACM, he swears, were against him right up to the top and they leaked everything to the NUM almost as soon as he had said it.

It became my experience very quickly that if more than two or three people knew about any decision that had been taken then so very quickly did Arthur Scargill. Such disloyalty seemed to be accepted with resignation by those around me. It was a fact of life in the fantasy world of Hobart House.

The conspiracy permeated the entire outfit right down to Harold Taylor (South Yorkshire Area Director) a non believer and Some colliery managers were like their counterparts in junior management at Hobart House somewhat upset with what we were doing.

His piece on NACODS reveals that Thatcher panicked and leading members of the Cabinet felt it was time to surrender; for himself he wanted to take them on, as he felt the Deputies and Overmen ought never to have been in Trade Unions in the first place. However, Thatcher told him he had to settle. In the event he admits quite frankly that he conned NACODS into thinking they had won the right of independent arbitration and review over the head of the NCB.

Through the fog of his paranoia it is still possible to see the enormous strengths of the strike, the success of the pickets. More importantly, he tells us that even by January 85, ten months after the start of the strike, 104 colliers stood and only 47 were working normally and after all the bluster he admits we came within a whisper of winning, and that's from the horse's mouth.

The Miners' Strike 1984/85 - Loss Without Limit by Martin Adeney and John Lloyd is perhaps the most unfactual work of all the recent 'authorities' on the strike, and yet standing as he does with great credit among the Kinnockites his book will be taken as the gospel.

The conclusion, indeed the theme of the book, is that we ought not to have fought, not in 84 and not in 26, the model for this period is the EETPU. Our fight was too rough, and unbalanced the preconceived idea of social harmony and an end to class conflict. He almost gloats on the casualties and lays them at the door of Arthur Scargill who he is convinced invented the entire dispute. Labour history is to Lloyd an unnecessary string of defeats and battles led by stupid people and followed by poor souls who knew no better. Consensus with the ruling class is, it seems, and always has been, from the time they took our children underground to the days when they clubbed our old people in their own homes, the only real way of advancing social progress. Such

94

a view among journalists is bread and butter material, among historians it is a long discredited theory. It certainly has no place in the Labour Movement no matter how broad one draws the definition.

Miner Conflicts, Major Contradictions, a Situationist / Autonomist / councilist work, uses *Socialist Worker*, a so-called Marxist paper, as its source of information. Later other anarchist papers will quote from *Miner Conflicts*, and so it goes on until the myth becomes a well-known statement of fact and beyond all doubt.

Even if the media bills Scargill as extremist he clearly has much in common with Edward Heath, the former PM. Both of them have realised how trade unionism is the enemy of the real unity of the proletariat which rears its violent head every time the masses of individuals band together against work, against forced unemployment, and against being policed, bossed about and insulted by two-faced functionaries

It is sufficient, it seems, simply to say it, it requires no explanation let alone a justification, Arthur is a Trade Union leader, therefore he is ipso facto a two-faced functionary.

Nowadays, Scargill's rhetoric doesn't sound even as daring as these creeps (TU leaders in 26). Everyone can be completely sure of that, just so long as they let him, he'll end up. . . .selling a demoralised defeat to his followers, possibly in order to get them to participate in an election for the bosses of the Labour Party, but certainly to preserve his miserable role of House Rebel in the decomposition of the capitalist economy.

This, remember, of a man who stood four square with the rank and file for 12 months of long struggle, refusing to bend to every possible manipulative device put to cow him or seduce him. Likewise he refused to play the role of 'class traitor' and 'sell out' which some sections of 'the left' had made out for him almost from the first week of the strike. The reality of Arthur Scargill's leadership like the reality of the strike itself, contradicts the stereotyped and preordinated lines down which the comrades in the armchairs predicted it would go. Making the wrong theory and predictions fit the facts is a bit like Cinderella's slipper on the ugly sister.

The pamphlet goes on to berate the miners for their loyalty to their elected leader (singing 'Arthur Scargill,' etc.). The authors of the pamphlet think this singing of Arthur's name is a Yorkshire phenomenon and incredibly enough explain it thus: *they reinforce not only the idea of the regionalism and parochialism of the Yorkshire miners, over developed by the rising success of many Yorkshire football teams and which helps the bosses divide and rule.* With such drivel as an alternative it is little wonder Arthur's sense of things comes over with crystal clarity by comparison.

Whereas the social democratic left and Euro communists tried to blame Arthur for dreaming up the whole strike and organising it single-handed (against everyone's wishes) this crowd say the opposite, i.e. Arthur had been opposed to a strike at the beginning. Our enemy's apparent enemy - in this case Scargill is no friend.

That many Nottingham miners have Polish family connections - as high as 50% in Ollerton - is certainly one of the reasons why they've not come out on strike. (*Freedom*) Presumably this is the reason why Walenska pinned his flag to the mast of Thatcher and called her the best Prime Minister in Europe and condemned the miners and Scargill 'for going too far and threatening the elected government.' Presumably it's the reason why both the official Polish Dock Workers' Union and the Solidarity variety refused to black the scab fuel to Britain, and cashed in on the extra bonus payments from the increased shipments. Or it could be that unlike the Polish miners in Doncaster who struck solid and picketed and at times were badly beaten by the police, and who stayed out until the last day, that the Polish miners in Notts, like the Geordie miners or Scottish miners in Notts (by and large) were spineless scabs. Our Anarchist pamphleteers refracting their own political differences with Arthur's defence of the 'workers' state', attribute the scabbing to Arthur's politics. At one point up to 40% of Nottingham miners were voluntarily on strike and in support of the strike, the heroic minority who stuck it out to the end faced victimisation and isolation unexperienced in the solidly striking areas.

Repeating another of the SWP's popular myths our armchair Anarchist insurgents then stand the facts on end and declare *A large section of miners were deliberately sent to Nottingham when the first battles of Orgreave were getting off the ground, thus helping the cops to maintain the thin blue line.* They can't blame Arthur for this, of course, since he supported the drive for Orgreave against the Yorkshire areas' resistance, this must put them on a spot as to who to support. That aside the truth of what happened is outlined in the earlier part of this book, but the strategy of going into Notts away from the expected raids on Orgreave was precisely the opposite of what they say, it was to thin the thick blue line thinner, and stop police concentrations whilst maximising our own.

As to the massive poverty of literature which has come out from the 'Soft Left,' 'Euro-Communist' and all positions 'Left Academic' since the strike, with all its sagely nodding academic agreement that we were quite wrong to struggle as we did, a new pamphlet could be filled simply with their disgraceful posturing. From the self described 'Anarchists' to the 'Communists' to Neil Kinnock's 'Man from the Lodge' (we think it was Ian Paisley) they either miss the point, or argue the age-old point, that the working class cannot and should not fight back without the recent structure of Parliamentary voting and surrendering of all action to a package of MPs or lawyers, all within the safe frame of the British Capitalist System. The Miners' action threatened them all. We could review all books since the strike, all articles such as the outpourings of (the Reverend!) Jimmy Reed, etc., but perhaps just one characterises them all - John Lloyd, current editor of the *New Statesman*. This is the intellectual exponent of 'An End to Class War,' as such he is the darling of the 'Soft Left,' and 'Creeping Euro Communist Factions.' He has become the 'balanced' view of the strike. . . .and many more strikes before including 1926 and all other sectors' strikes and struggles as well. It was illustrative that Lloyd, entering the field of history from his muddy path of journalism, dismissed all primary evidence, never researched any of the work of our communities (of which there are now dozens), and never interviewed any of the activists such as outlined in this book, indeed used only the tight hall of mirrors already built by other journalists and himself.

This book will not be a surprise to Lloyd, the facts were never a surprise - they simply did not and will not fit in so they are left out, in the interests of the status quo. Among academics perhaps the earthy plodgy style of Lloyd's book might keep him in good stead; among the people engaged in this struggle, the young 'uns, the women and the miners his outpourings have no meaning in their actual history. It was because of people like him that they set down to write their own histories of what happened, what went on, how they felt and how proud they were to be there. People change society, people will determine what they need to do in any required situation and neither law, the organs of oppression or the grave robbers who turn up when the bodies are being counted, will ever alter that material fact of history. For historians of the future, sorting through the mass of material you will find on this colossal dispute we advise, take note of the actors on the stage and what they said, and not the critics who sat in the gallery concerned by other things as the play went on.

The Left and the Miners

The problem for the left is their eternal dilemma, to make reality fit their preconceived theory of reality. So it is that real situations in which ordinary people are involved become shoehorned into or abstracted out of "the real situation" in order that the lefty theory might fit. How ordinary folk see the struggle for themselves, what are their objectives, what are their inherited, adopted or developed means by which these objectives are pursued; in almost all cases such things are brushed aside, yes, by the Leninist left, but also by situationists and some anarchists. Brushed aside in order that "the real lessons", "the real goals" are followed. By and large, the Left appears not only with a different agenda, or certainly a larger agenda, that the one being debated by folk in struggle, but also comes amongst us "as it were afire" with the prescriptions of how to achieve their agenda.

I remember quite vivdly a scene at the Durham Miners' Gala, as an elderly pitman listened patiently as a very young member of the Workers' Revolutionary Party explained: "Now here's why you lost the 1926 strike. . . ." Of course the point of the lesson, like all the other lessons, is that they lost because the WRPer and his party wasn't around to tell the stupid miners where they were going wrong!

But the vanguards are selfless! Should the struggle break from the factory or pit, should it crash kicking and fighting into the street, they're straight there, lad, flooding in with an armful of papers to explain to us, the people in struggle, whose struggle it is in the first place, just where we're going wrong! Now frequently not only are our methods wrong, doomed, reformist, or else ultra-leftist, economist, or adventurist, individual terrorist even, we also often take part in the wrong struggle anyway. We shouldn't be doing what we're doing, we've got it all wrong and we should be doing something entirely different. There is never any significance to the struggles of the workers themselves, until the Leninist / Situationist / Trotskyist Moses comes along and tells us what it is. It's like Billy Connolly's sarcastic vision of the primitive jungle tribe standing around saying "I wish an explorer would come and tell us where we are." So the workers generally bumble through history saying, "I wish the revolutionary leadership would turn up and tell us what we're doing!"

And yet such theories of organisation and practice are generally cobbled together in somebody's backyard and then wheeled onto the street and sold to the working class as "their organisation", despite the fact that the working class has not previously seen it and certainly played no part in its construction.

Can you wonder that industrial and unionised workers identify more with their Trade Union branch, lodge, shop stewards committee or whatever, than they do with the revolutionary donkey constructed out of somebody's Book of Revolutionary Organisation.This is not so much "blind faith in reformist organisation" as identification with organisations that have been built by the workers themselves, and although deformed to a greater or lesser extent by bureaucracy and treachery, are still the front line defence of the workers, who will use them and test them to breaking point far more efficiently than the home grown do-it-yourself variety constructed by the SWP or the RCP, for example.

To contrast, for example, the National Union of Mineworkers, or its forebears, the Miners' Federation of Great Britain & Ireland, and the Miners' Union - the best part of 180 years of unbroken class struggle trade unionism - with the will o' the wisp nature of most left groups seems an uneven contest. Which has greater utility to the class, which has more loyalty from the class?

One could go further and point to specific areas of the miners' union's history where it has been a class leader and a catalyst in revolutionary upsurges....the 1830s through to the 1860s as part of the Swing revolts, as cornerstones of the Chartist Movement....1912 and the industrial General Strike wave....1926....1972/74....and of course the strike of 1984/85.

Despite this when we launched our defensive assault against the full weight of the state, as a community and an industrial union, the left came, not to fall in behind, nor yet to assist when we needed them. . . .they came to lead us and tell us what we should do. What were their credentials for telling us what to do? Despite the bureaucracy (albeit a left one) and despite certain privileged sections of the union structure, what made their so-called revolutionary organisations more revolutionary than our Trade Union in practice? We are still waiting to be convinced.

The Socialist Workers' Party, despite a venomously anti-union verbiage, strangely shares the same bureaucratic lack of vision and faith in the workers as do the NUM bureaucrats. To this day they don't really understand the tactics employed in the 84/85 strike and never really grasped the pickets' perspective of the struggle. Instead they basked in the reflected glow of Arthur Scargill's General Custer impersonation. - Never mind the tactics, charge! - whilst they were determined to fight to the last drop of our blood, we wished to shed that blood less freely, more wisely, not less revolutionary, certainly no less violently if it meant retaliating against the police (or retaliating first against the police!), just more tactically. If the different perspectives can be summed up in military terms, Arthur and the SWP saw themselves as the van of the class army lined up against the ruling class enemy in a do-or-die battle at Orgreave. . . . we saw ourselves as a guerilla force of rarely more than 20,000 pickets nationally, fighting a massive deployment of police with the full range of computer and surveillance equipment. Standing toe to toe we would always be battered, so we used guerilla tactics; blocking the M1, hit squad raids on scab pits or police bases, blocking the Humber Bridge; ruse tactics to draw the mass of police off somewhere else while our main force deployed to some least-expected power station, wharf or scab pit. Because of the absolute need for secrecy only the elected picket co-ordinators knew the plan, village pits had posters on the walls; "Keep Picket Targets Secret! The Walls Have Ears!"

These targets drove the SWP to distraction, because they didn't know where the action was until after we'd been and gone and done it! This is very troubling if you're a vanguard! Arthur was similarly distressed but he also had no control or say over the direction of our targets or the manner with which we conducted these attacks. We also differed on perceptions of the struggle. Arthur saw Orgreave as a Saltley Gate, a rally point for the whole Trade Union movement and the Left; mass enough of our class together and we could swamp them. This strategy was fatally flawed, not least because we'd tried it at Grunwick and despite far more support than the miners got, had still lost, we'd tried it at Warrington and got battered to hell. For things had changed since Saltley, not simply the responses or lack of them from union bureaucracies and often from union members, but also the degree to which the police had been given their head and told not to back off. Even had we been prepared to bleed long enough we would always ultimately lose that kind of head to head battle, at least so long as we remained unarmed. . . .and even then I wouldn't imagine us marching with flags flying and bayonets fixed to a field of battle which had previously marked out and set up by an even more armed police force. It shouldn't need arguing that our tactics were wiser, more radical and more daring. . . .they were also more fun. "Everyone to Orgreave" was not a tactic, it was an act of faith or at best a case of misjudgment. What it also was was the restoration of a tactic in which the self-designated leaders could start playing vanguard again.

Of course Arthur had "had the vision" and, the Great Plan formed in his head, he announced off his own bat on every TV channel in the land that everyone worth their salt should go to Orgreave.

We went.

Why?

I remember one Mayday in Glasgow debating with fellow republicans how best to take the cause of Ireland onto the Mayday march and onto those streets of mixed traditions. We agreed that by confining the question to Troops and Out and Self Determination for the Irish people, we would outflank the Trades Council bureaucracy and the heavy Stickie presence. But one of our number, despite our logic, our tactics or our majority, said he would raise the Irish Tricolour, emblazoned with the Phoenix of the Provisional IRA. Of course we knew that once he did that he would be attacked by the Orangies, the Stalinists, the Trades Council bureaucrats and we would have no choice but to defend him, and the flag, against them.

The same principled obligation was placed on us by Arthur's "Horatio on the Bridge" stance. Ditch warfare, the replay of World War 1, had started at Orgreave, the fight was happening, and we had no choice but to join it. Fiercely and unrestrained, publically uncritical, but we knew it to be foolish in the extreme. The left viewed it like the Charge of the Light Brigade - bloody but magnificent.

Not that, once they got there, they actually did anything! Did this revolutionary left that had shouted "Orgreave" on our marches actually have a plan once we got there. . . ? Oh no. . . .off you chaps go and do the fighting as best you can and we'll sell papers telling you how well or bad you've done.

To my dying day I'll never forget the scene, as Hatfield and Armthorpe miners, the then storm troops of the pickets, launched a fearful physical assault, semi-naked and unarmed, against the massed ranks of riot shields. . . .despite the police armoury the sheer weight, determination and boisterousness of the pickets knocked line upon line of police shields over. . . .and then the whistle blew, the shields stood to the side, and a mounted cavalry of nightstick wielding armoured thugs rode forth. . . .we retreated up the road. . . .and as we did so passed a lone man trying to sell us Workers' Power. "Workers' Power!" he cried, as we ran past, bleeding, sweating and laughing. Then the cavalry rode past him, to the left and right as bombards of bricks hit them from all sides. We retreated into the trees and waited till they rode back, bloody and hot. Then we crept out to dare again. . . .and found the man unmoved in his central position. "Workers' Power!" he cried. . . .The class war literally took place all around him; he was like a programme seller at a concert, not part of the band, nor yet part of the audience, he was estranged from both; just a seller of a version of events of which he was not a part. Fine, I was a 60s product, if that's your thing, man, but does he really think either we, or the cops for that matter, needed to read the paper? Though I'm not sure if he didn't try to sell the cavalry a copy. Maybe for a front page photo of the charge, I mean the cops probably thought they looked magnificent. They certainly thought Workers' Power were insignificant. So did we.

The Workers' Revolutionary Party operates in the revolutionary Hall of Mirrors which decrees that all workers' struggles are doomed without they are led by the Revolutionary Party, namely themselves. So it then follows that anything the working class do is doomed, a blind alley, because it hasn't been led by them. For people like myself, field officers of the struggle, it was automatic that we would wish to betray the struggle, because we weren't part of the revolutionary party. Mass picketing, hit squads, anti-scab, anti-police assaults were all a dead end, they said. Instead they offered us a real solution; the miners should call on the TUC General Council to lead a general strike! We replied. . . .woah, woah, we're the miners! Don't you know anything at all about our history? The TUC? A general strike? Are the WRP that stupid? No, stupidity is their public face. In private they'll tell you they know the TUC will never organise a general strike and if they did they'd only betray it as they did in 1926. So why call for it?

Because us dumbchucks, the rank and file pitmen and our families, and the workers at large need to be shown that the existing trade union structure is no good for this sort of battle and it should be left to the revolutionary party.

Got it? Urge us into a defeat, we get smashed, then pick up the pieces to build up your own outfit by blaming it on the old outfit. Nice. Trouble with this theory is, we'd been there in 1926. Miners' children are weaned on the story of that betrayal of the miners by the TUC. We grew up knowing the limitations of the TUC General Council and that's why we would never accept that stupid slogan of the WRP. If this was a sample of their organisational worth to the NUM, is it any wonder the NUM continued the struggle with fire and pride whilst the WRP stood under umbrellas for fear of the rain and tried pathetically to sell us wet papers you couldn't even light the fire with!

So what is the point or relevance of all this? Simply that the NUM, as a tried and tested organ of the miners for generations, despite its designation as a trade union, is not simply a trade union and need not remain so if the members of that organisation wish to extend it to wider and more political fields. This can be done formally through the changing of rules and organs; more usually it is done by building (constitutionally) unofficial committees, councils, joint branch panels, assemblies etc. This is not done in opposition to the NUM, which we hold as our organisation, but in extension of it. It is because the trade union form has limitations, not least from dire anti-union laws, that we recognise in many cases what functions are best served through other forms, which although not part of the structure of the NUM overlap or criss-cross it. Thus desite the existence of formal union committees, nearly every pit had a strike committee, formed of strike activists; often these included representatives of the womens' support groups, sections of the unemployed etc. It is these who plan the implementation of picket tactics and the "extra-curricular" activity which nobody claims yet is still organised in and around the committees and the union. Unofficial gatherings of local branches or panels elect strike co-ordinators who will, quite outside the formal union structure, draw up targets and plans of attack and initiatives. And yet at the same time this is a strike of the NUM, and every man and woman proudly proclaims their loyalty to its form. Their direct organisation, their fuller participation, their community based,

104

activist oriented extensions of the formal union were not and are not contradictory. At least we understand them. The Leninist with his vision of the trade union as an obstacle to the struggle cannot be that flexible.

Take for example a recent struggle in the Yorkshire coalfield; Frickley Colliery on strike over a dismissed comrade. The strike must spread, but anti-union laws hamstring the formal union apparatus. How does the rank and file member of the union view the situation? He is both loyal to the NUM and yet because of the restrictions placed upon its formal structures by the law, is inhibited from their use. He declares, send unofficial pickets, and we will not pass them. The branch cannot formally sanction this legally, but branch officials declare union policy of not crossing picket lines. They say, it's my formal duty to tell you that such action is secondary picketing and unlawful, the men say, OK, then go home, and the branch officials go with them. The SWP on the other hand demand, make the leaders act, they call for us to send formal resolutions to the official NUM Council Meeting, knowing full well the Area Officials will rule them out of order, for if they didn't the whole organisation would be smashed in the courts. Both we and the Area Officials, on a nod and wink, say get on with the strike by other means and ignore the formal structure. All of us involved understand that this is a pantomime intended to let us do what want to do anyway. . . .the SWP sees it as some serious Shakespearean drama, and assumes the idea is to confront the union apparatus. It isn't, it's to confront British Coal's apparatus, stick 2 fingers up at the law and fight for the reinstatement of the sacked Frickley comrade.

We have need of the formal structure of the NUM for welfare benefits, for countless legal injury and death cases. So we maintain it, at the same time going around it, over it or underneath it to do what we want to. We see this as no contradiction. The SWP thinks we have it wrong, because frankly they don't understand our relationship with official and unofficial aspects of our organisation. But as a matter of fact, why should they?

As things turned out, the Frickley strike, largely because the unofficial flying pickets weren't deployed, and a different device aimed at using the law while breaking it failed. In all, we, the members, kept the official union out of it, because they couldn't assist us. The SWP blamed the collapse of the strike on the failure of the leaders to act.

We pass each other like ships in the night.

Not that such blinkered vision is confined to Leninists. Cajo Brendel, in Autonomous Class Struggle in Britain 1945/77, what I suppose is a situtationist work [in fact Cajo Brendel is not a situationist, but a veteran Dutch council communist], misses the relationship of the worker to the trade union in a period of mass trade union upsurge, sees all struggle as anti-union and non-struggle as trade unionism. He repeats the dogma that unions can only restrict the struggle of the class and never, not ever, have been used by the class as a combative force, despite bureaucratic restrictions and outright betrayals. He is confident enough to write an extensive thesis without once referring to any of the workers involved in the struggles he cites. The struggle is an abstract, it doesn't involve real people with their own views on things and their own ways of changing things.

And herein lies the rub.

Organisations are composed of individuals. These individuals are involved in actual class war, not for some theoretical reason, or some moral reason, but in order to meet the needs of social survival, and in order to resist the exploitation placed on them by capitalist society. These people acting as a class have built self-defence organisations, trade unions for example. Over the years, and in some cases from the very start, these organisations have become bureaucratic, conservative and obstructive. . . .this has not stopped workers using them, making them fight, and literally picking them up kicking and screaming and forcing them to act. Often they have built unofficial sections, semi-official sections, sometimes they work within or without the organisation, sometimes they use the organisation as a jumping off board for activities far beyond the normal perception of what a trade union does. Dropping concrete on blackleg buses for example, or burning them, launching petrol bomb attacks on police stations. . . .in 1984. Or derailing the Flying Scotsman in 1926. . . .though that was after a formal resolution to that effect was accepted by the Chopwell Lodge! Workers will make these organisations do what they wish, or fight to make them do what they wish. They will drive the trade union bus in whatever direction they want to go, no matter what it says on the front. And while it wasn't constructed for, say, charging police roadblocks, from time to time it is the nearest thing to hand and will do until something stronger comes along. This bus may not take us as far as we want to go. . . .but in many cases we can take it as far as it will go, at which point we'll adapt it or change it for something else.

People make history. People make the means of class war and are far more versatile and inspirational than the Leninist or Situationist who sees all forms carved in tablets of stone, unchanging, fixed, regardless of circumstances. This determinism would please a Jehovah's Witness. We say, the future is unwritten, this is true, but the means by which we write it, draw it, shape it, or spell it will be determined as we go. Also if the future is unwritten, the means we write it with are also not predetermined.

For us as revolutionaries, we should intervene in the struggles the workers are themselves engaged in, we should assist them in the way they wish to be assisted. We should put our determination, skill, constructive and destructive abilities at their disposal, and ask, how can we assist you? How are we better placed to do some of the things you want doing but can't do yourselves? We must fundamentally recognise that the working class was engaged in struggle before any of us organisationally or individually came along. They are engaged in struggle now, with us or without us, they are not waiting for us. If we wish to assist the struggle we should join it. We should fight where they are fighting, if necessary in the unions they are fighting in, or the tenants' committee they are fighting in, or the anti-pollution campaign they are fighting in, or the anti-motorway group they are fighting in. We will be of relevance as long as we intervene, without preconditions, without delusions of vanguardism, into the actual struggles of the working class, not standing outside the class mocking the crude attempts at combat organisation the workers have built, but alongside them, as part of them.

In the words of the Internationale:
No saviours from on high deliver
The chains our own right hands shall sever.

GLOSSARY

The words and acronyms explained below may be unfamiliar to many people. Some of them are alphabet soup from the union movement, others normal speech in the north of England, others specific to the mining industry.

ACAS
Advisory, Conciliation and Arbitration Service. Began in 1974 with its legal basis embodied in the Employment Protection Act 1975. Government financed, although ostensibly independent; its objective was to find solutions to disputes without recourse to strikes, lock-outs or the law.

afters
One of the 3 or 4 shift colliery cycle. Beginning at 12 noon nd finishing at 7.15pm one could be in the boozer by 8pm and still be confident of a good 8 hours' sleep before work.

APEX
Association of Professional, Executive, Clerical and Computer Staff. A 'trade' union which ultimately undermined the industrial union COSA, a section of the NUM, by breaking the industrial link between white coller office staff and miners.

ASLEF
Associated Society of Locomotive Engineers and Firemen.

AUEW
Amalgamated Union of Engineering Workers.

BACM
British Association of Colliery Managers.

bait
Snap, piece, the 20 minutes in the middle of the shift when miners take a food break of whatever sandwiches they've brought.

bray
Ancient, probably British Celtic expression meaning to heavily bang something.

BSC
British Steel Corporation.

Coal House
The NCB multi-storey office block and HQ in the centre of Doncaster. Scenes of violent picketing as scab office workers worked despite coal industry strike action in 72, 74, and 84/85. Now closed owing to pit closures!

COSA
Colliery Officials and Staffs Association. The white collar section (covering safety staff, training staff and office workers) of the NUM.

dint
When coal or stone is emoved underground nature at once wishes to close the hole up again. Often this is done from downwards weight pressure. At other times it comes from below, and the earth boils up. A dint is the operation of removing the 'floor below' or rock intrusion.

EETPU
Electrical, Electronic, Telecommunications and Plumbing Union.

gaan canny
Lowlands dialect meaning go easily. In the context of mining it is a go slow with the object of reducing production while still getting paid.

gis
Give me.

Hobart House
The NCB/British Coal national HQ and administration centre in London.

lowse
Meaning to knock off. Lowlands dialect, literally "loose", it comes from the ancient days of mining when the rope was lowsed from the corps used in drawing up the coal. The rope was then slung into "arseloops"

in which groups of colliers sat or hung and were drawn up the shaft. "She's lowse!" was the shout signifying the end of the shift.

M&Q
The Mines and Quarries Act (1954). The stringent safety legislation embodying over 100 years of safety regulations in mines and quarries. In November 1993 the Tory government repealed it in favour of a loose "code of practice" in order to allow private mine operators to operate more cheaply, ie less safely.

marras
Workmates on the same shift or on the same stall.

NACODS
National Association of Colliery Overmen, Deputies and Shotfirers.

nowt
Nothing.

panel
Semi-official collective of miners' branches in the four traditional districts of Yorkshire. Set up simply to hear the executive committee reports, they became self-governing, co-ordinating bodies for many unofficial actions.

pegged
Stuck in a particular place.

Red Hills
The HQ of the Durham miners' union.

rag up
A Yorkshire expression for walking off the job in wildcat action. The "rags" are the old clothes miners wear down the pit.

red ragging
Red raggers is a Yorkshire expression teams and individuals particularly prone to ragging up when aggrieved. It implies a political motivation.

110

Saltley Gate
The massive coal depot in Birmingham from which scab lorries were shipping coal for distribution in 72. A trial of strength took place between flying pickets and police, attempting to shut down or keep open the depot. It was a contest the miners won when engineering and transport workers from all over Birmingham downed tools and literally marched to join the miners.

stand
In the context of "let the coalfield stand" it means to halt production.

welfare centres
Pit villages like wild west towns were built in the middle of nowhere. Suddenly faced with large influxes of migrant miners and their families, facilities for social and recreational purposes became an imperative for many mine owners fearful of the disorder which marked 17th century mining areas. In collaboration with the miners' union extensive welfare facilities were developed over the years.

Last Word

By 23rd November 93, it had been made public that British Coal would solve the problem of the Doncaster miners by closing the remaining Doncaster pits, Frickley, Bentley and Hatfield. The sole surviving Goldthorpe Colliery was known to be coming to an end owing to seam exhaustion. The same day the last pit in Doncaster was given a date for closure, so too was the last pit in Durham. The decimation, now relentless, is laying waste to whole mining areas, and our industry and union, once so massive and imposing, lie in ruins, victims of the class war. To many of us the meaning of our lives is so much the poorer, though we have no regrets that we made the stand and took on the state. In the words of the statement issued from the final mass meeting of Hatfield Main NUM Branch:-

"We know that wherever the Doncaster miners go, whatever they do, they will keep proud to our heritage; always joining the appropriate union, never crossing a picket line of any workers in dispute.

Exhausted and demoralised, the present has been taken from us; the past and future, however, belong to us and we shall guard them jealously. Mr Houghton, John Major, Margaret Thatcher and the rich folk you represent, this moment is yours - but you shall never take from us our dignity as workers who have fought for justice and a better world. You may disperse us from this spot, this moment in time, but our conviction shall remain wherever we go and in the generations of post-miners children who follow us.

THE FUTURE IS OURS!"

27th November 93